United Credit

Prosperity without Money

By Jonathon Ray Spinney

United Credit

First Printing March 2013

Red Bear Press
192 Main Street, Suite 8
Ellsworth, Maine 04605

ISBN 978-1-4675-6225-6

Book Design:
Birdwalk Studio
Blue Hill, ME

Printed in The USA

Dedication

This book is dedicated to all those who are working towards a truly humanitarian transformation of all human economic activity on this blue star of Earth.

It is with many regrets that I am selling this book for "money"; however, all profits will go towards building the United Credit Foundation and helping to build new economic prosperity without money.

Table of Contents

INTRODUCTION

What is proposed in the following pages is an economic philosophy; a new economic system, which I believe our nation and perhaps the world desperately needs. Why the title "United Credit"? America is a country that is currently surviving because of credit. Credit saturates and supports our national economy as well as International economies. Credit saturates the economies of states, cities and towns. It saturates the lives of all Americans. We are united by credit! It chains us to our lives. It controls the markets, our banks, our businesses, our health care and ultimately, our freedom. Every aspect of our society is driven by credit. It is time to challenge and transform our conceptions of "credit" and move away from our debt driven economy.

Imagine for a moment a "credit" system without money, without bills and without debt: **United Credit**.

Our country is in trouble. Americans, as human souls, as Earth citizens, are in trouble. We are rapidly descending into an abyss of uncontrollable debt, loss of values, unhappiness and emptiness. We have lost touch with our hearts and with the rest of the world. We have nearly lost our humanity and are in need of a whole new way of surviving the coming collapse of capitalism. Capitalism has always had its own demise in sight, its own doom built inherently into its basic philosophy and existence. To acquire for greater and greater personal gain, to allow unending corporate growth, to expand to the ends of the Earth and to the ends of materialism is a system that has no light or hope in the end. It is a system that leads to spiritual and environmental death and destruction—swallowing up all the resources of the world without regard or consideration for anyone or anything. Capitalism is not freedom and today, world communities are realizing that it's not anything that humanity could possibly sustain.

What is needed is an economic system that is built on compassion for all humans—a system that is built on sharing rather than taking, on giving rather than acquiring, on helping rather than withholding. What is needed is an economic system that respects our limited resources on this planet—that respects all the living creatures and natural systems that keep us alive and healthy. What is needed is an economic system that respects each other and our children—our future generations. Most important of all—we need an economic system that not only rids us of **debt** but one that does not allow debt creation.

I believe that there is a solution right now and, in the following pages, a solution to the crisis that we have created will be presented. But, as you read on, keep an open mind—keep an open heart and I think you might possibly relate to the proposal of "United Credit–Prosperity without Money".

Part 1

United Credit and Economic Philosophy

Prosperity without Money

Imagine a world where all human beings can live, eat, work, learn, explore, enjoy life, share and be happy without money. Imagine a credit card that never has a billing statement—a credit card that you can never have cancelled and yet, a credit card that you could eventually use for all your needs: In other words, a credit card without **debt**! It's not an impossible dream. All things in this world have come from imagination and dream. Someone first imagined every aspect of our lives—the table we sit at or the car we drive. We are living in a world that is a kaleidoscope of everyone else's dreams. It's time for a new concept of economic prosperity; a dream that is truly humanitarian; a dream that desires economic prosperity for all people—not just a select few. Prosperity **without** money is a possible reality but the possibility lies in one belief and fundamental value: helping others.

It's time to radically transform our conceptions about money and "credit". Rather than debt creation, credit should be understood as something all people are entitled to—something that they deserve by being part of the human community here on Earth. United Credit, from its beginning, would be a foundation totally based on helping each other. I am not proposing a barter system. I am proposing something much greater—a radical change in our beliefs and in our actions—a leap forward in trust and faith to a time of peace and widespread prosperity on this planet.

Unfortunately, it would require money to create a system without money. We have to start somewhere. Currently, our system of money has no real value. It has only an artificial or forced value—*fiat money* (money that is no longer tied to gold or anything concrete or substantial). In 1971, our government shifted to fiat money. Since most of the economies in the Western world were tied to the US economy, their monetary base also switched to fiat. Before this, the value of money was tied to gold, silver or some kind of commodity. Our currency today has no real value. It's just printed paper. All money-supported "prosperity" that is enjoyed by the developed world today is a false prosperity. Thus, to create "Prosperity without Money" really means creating a true and meaningful economic value system linked to something real—**human actions**!

We have to start somewhere. It's going to take money to create a system without money. We are going to have to gradually dissolve the money or false value system we currently rely on as new economic value systems and real prosperity are created. We are going to have to dissolve the debt mentality that has been forced on our society by the banking industry and the Federal Reserve. *(The Federal Reserve, contrary to its name, is a central bank owned by private individuals. These individuals control our government as well as all the banks in this country—controlling us through expanding cycles of debt.)*

Over the last few years, while I was writing this book, our government has put many trillions of dollars into a futile attempt to bailout our collapsing economy and prop up the fake fiat currency—*money*. Perhaps a couple of hundred billion dollars could be designated for a United Credit fund. Alternatively, a United Credit could be established in other ways such as endowments and donations. Once such a fund is established as well as an infrastructure and system to manage it, every American would then have the opportunity to apply for a United Credit card. However, the cards will not have any value until each person builds credit on their card. Every aspect of our society is in need of help—hospitals, road and bridge construction, elderly care systems, schools, etc. As people give their time and skills to these needs, they build credit.

It is the people who are in real need right now who can make use of this the most. Money from the fund would be turned into credit as things actually get done, as people actually are helped. The person who lost his or her job two months ago and cannot pay their mortgage needs help right now! They need help combined with a method of building pride and dignity. The current social welfare and unemployment systems do not help to build any aspect of personal self-worth.

This whole era of "unemployment" is one of the negative creations of capitalism and global corporate expansion and it is a false reality that societies have been duped into. The infrastructure of the American landscape is badly in need of upgrades, transformation and sustainable change. American society itself is crumbling due to increasing apathy, isolation and despair. The fact is that there are potential jobs at every level of our society that could enrich and empower individuals and communities.

Every single community in this nation and around the world has the potential to create meaningful jobs for every one of their citizens. All that is needed is a new economic model—a new way of managing community wealth and resources as well as a new way of compensation for human service—all within a unified vision for a better and more sustainable future for all. *Current capitalist economic models are ones that take (steal) community resources, community wealth, community pride and dignity.* NO person, in any community who is willing to help others and work, should ever be "unemployed" nor should they ever be denied their basic economic rights: food, shelter, etc.

Now, I know that this all sounds somewhat idealistic, but I think a new economic model such as United Credit would offer hope. For instance, say I lose my job. Rather than sitting home depressed, I can go help out at a homeless shelter, give rides to the elderly or offer my time, abilities or skills in a meaningful way to others. My United Credit card is validated with credit at an extremely fair exchange. The hours I have given to help others or the hours I work serving a greater cause than myself are reflected as credit (units of **human service value**) on my United Credit card. I can now pay my mortgage or buy groceries. But most importantly, I have given something of myself, I have overcome my own needs to help others and I feel better about myself. That is the KEY to this whole idea. It is this aspect of the plan that will help change the philosophy in our country about money and economics.

Currently, so many people in this country have no way to improve their lives—no opportunity to work. So many people in desperate need have no way to change their situations—no way to even begin to realize that they have something to give. *Everyone* has something to give. Even the homeless person on the street needing a place to sleep can give something to earn a bed. It is a step forward. When you help someone, you are helping yourself. Once a national database of places and organizations that need help and volunteers is created, anyone will be able to access it at any time and from any place.

Basically, the funds backing United Credit would go directly to the people who are not only in need of it, but to those who are willing to give something of themselves to earn it. Even children could come into the system at any age once able and willing to contribute to society. Can you imagine a world in one generation from now if children are provided with such a new economic model?

Taking this one step further, companies could also be issued a United Credit card. Some of their work and employee activity could be given to those in need—to local and national rebuilding projects or to the needs of others in foreign countries. For example, an American company could provide their services in Africa creating clean energy, clean water systems or by supplying farming supplies. The company would receive a fair credit toward their United Credit account for the contribution. In addition, employees involved with the contribution of their time and skills would receive United credit. United Credit would reward the company, which would in turn reward the employees—all within a normal 40 hour week. In this way, the philosophy and system is expanded little by little. *Companies that move quickly towards developing new energy systems or promoting humanitarian causes could be given special consideration by United Credit.*

United Credit would reward real change, real action and real deeds.

Now, obviously, you cannot keep indefinitely funding a program like this. As United Credit expand and grows, it would become a moral issue for those of great wealth to give to the system. The main objective of United Credit would be to create economic units of value that replace money thus creating prosperity through new economic activity—taking fiat wealth and turning it into human resource and humanitarian wealth. All acquired material resources would lose their monetary value and be given a humanitarian value. The expansion of United

Credit will eventually happen **without money**, as the following pages will reveal.

Everybody is dependent on the service sector of our country: public maintenance, firefighters, maids, waiters and waitresses, etc. The people who make up the service sector are the people in the most need. However, the wealthy are in need too. They are in need of moral and spiritual help. Considering the desperate state of the world today, it truly is a moral and spiritual issue for the wealthy to begin to share—not only of their wealth but also of their time and energy. United Credit would not only provide opportunities and help to those in need, it would provide opportunities for others to share their wealth. The worst thing that can happen to any person with financial wealth is to become removed from the plight of those in the society that provided the means to that wealth (working classes). All wealth comes with a social cost.

As United Credit foundation grows and expands, as individuals in need offer what talents and skills they have, or their human resources, and as the businesses, suppliers, farmers, and providers come into the foundation, the exchange of money would begin to diminish. There are millions of empty homes in this country that have been foreclosed upon. There are millions of used and new cars sitting on lots around the country —a market that is completely saturated. There is excess in every sector of the American economy. The first and fundamental goal of United Credit would be to begin to acquire these excesses through donations, endowments, or purchases with funding. Then, these material resources would become available to people building their United Credit fund. Ultimately, a person giving their time, energy and skills fulltime to others in the United Credit system would not have a mortgage or car payment. They would be provided these resources to use—

not own. Communal (not State) ownership of these types of material resources is an important issue for United Credit and is discussed further in following chapters. Providing these types of resources to people in need without putting them into **debt** is not only possible but is the part of the foundation for economic transformation.

In the transition years of building the United Credit foundation, money would be an important asset. It will take money to pay businesses and services needed for individuals earning United Credit. Not all businesses and services will adapt to the foundation. In the beginning, it is realistic to assume very few would adopt or become a part of the foundation. For example, an individual who has built credit on his or her United Credit card may have an immediate need of dental work. However, there may be no dentist in the area that they live contributing to the United Credit foundation. United Credit would settle the bill as well as solicit the local dentists to become a part of the foundation.

In early 2009, a Southern Californian married couple lost their jobs simultaneously. They saw no hope and had no place to turn—no opportunity to immediately go someplace and give their time and energy to a cause in order to take care of their mortgage and family needs. They committed suicide and took with them their five children. It's a tragic situation that will likely be repeated again if our economic system continues on its present course. If a system such as United Credit had been in place and they had known about its benefits, I do not think they would have ever reached that point of desperation. They would have been able to keep their dignity, as United Credit would be a program of pride and dignity—not a welfare system! Eventually, United Credit could naturally transform or replace not only the unemployment system but also the welfare system.

United Credit, once established, would be the safety net for all Americans. United Credit would provide immediate access to a place or service that needs help and offer a way for individuals to pay their bills. United Credit will bring all of America together and match needs of individuals to needs of companies and organizations. All of this could be created without the personal exchange of money. United Credit would never send a bill to any American—only an available credit statement, and of course *available credit* would be based on real action, real giving and real sharing—real prosperity.

In the case of the California couple who committed suicide; if the hospital where they worked had been a part of a system like United Credit, they could have kept their jobs and perhaps, at the very least, done other jobs at the same hospital or another local hospital. United Credit could have stepped in to reimburse the hospital if needed until a solution could be found for the crisis. United Credit could have provided a database of many other organizations or institutions that were in need of their skills.

One of the areas that I feel United Credit would be very beneficial is the health care industry. For example, if all the maintenance, janitorial or kitchen jobs at health care facilities were filled with volunteers from the United Credit system, these facilities would save millions and would in turn be able to fund supplemental medical funding to those in need—those without insurance. A portion of their savings could also be put back into United Credit. Make it a win-win situation for everyone.

Doctors and nurses could be given extra incentives through United Credit to enter the system and give five hours a week at United Credit health care facilities. These centers would provide health care to those in need and, most importantly, to those who have established credit on their United Credit card through serving and giving to others. The allotment/deduction of credit to each doctor/patient based on their service to others would have to be done in a fair and proportionate way. I do not see this as a complicated problem. I see it as something that could be worked out easily.

There would of course have to be "grace credits" for those who are disabled, sick, handicapped, etc. I believe that there are many creative ways to fund that aspect of United Credit and make it work. There are people in this society who would have to shift from taking to giving. In their giving, they would receive. There is not one able bodied person alive today in our country that cannot give something of themselves. And there are countless organizations, infrastructure and social areas of need.

The next chapter is about ownership of the material world—about the fact that we really are all stewards of property or things while we are here. We don't take them with us when we pass over. In other chapters, I will develop ideas about how United Credit could become an immediate and long-term solution to the home mortgage crisis.

Right now, state and city budgets across this country are experiencing immense deficits. There are uncharted difficulties arising in areas of childcare, social services, municipal services and health care. United Credit would offer immediate assistance. It would bring people together to fill the gaps. United

Credit could now be set up as an emergency funding organization, but could evolve quickly into a new economic model.

There are a lot of social and economic, as well as political issues to contend with if such a program were to be implemented in this country. America needs to rebuild its dignity and pride. Americans need to rebuild their dignity and pride. In each of the following chapters, I will attempt to address the social, economic and political issues challenging a new model of prosperity without money.

What United Credit is proposing is a new unit of economic value as the basis of a new economy.

What we had in the past: the dollar (unit of value) equaled some measured fraction of gold. ***Gold symbolizes the ancient quest for wealth and power.***

What we shifted to in the early seventies: the dollar equaled what? There was nothing real to equate to the dollar. It was only the believed value that kept it seemingly real.

What United credit is proposing: credit (units of value) equal to real human action, deeds or service to others and society. What United Credit is proposing is a way for all people to live happy and fulfilling lives without creating endless cycles of debt.

FOR OTHERS IN THE END

Since I was a child, I have always marveled about the attachment that people, especially Americans, have to the material world. This world is ancient—millions and millions of years old. Humans are here for what—one second in the cosmic time frame? Our individual lives span an average of merely seventy or eighty years! The water molecules that are now in my body may someday be inside a tree in Australia. There is nothing permanent about my body or my life at all. Everything in the material world is interdependent and in a state of constant change. The permanent is beyond us. We are not material beings. We are spiritual beings in a material world—a world of flux and change.

Everything we create, everything we build, all that we try to hold on to will fade away someday into something else. What we create or build is always left for others in the end. Even when we are selfish and greedy, we are creating something that will not be ours in the end! Even if we do not want to share what we have in the present, we will share it when we pass over!

I do not mean to say that death is an end. However, it is an end to this one life—this one passage through the material world: a world that we are meant to use, share and take care of as we pass through. It is not my intention to discuss transitions of the soul, karma or reincarnation in this book. I will say however, that no matter what you believe about the nature of the soul, about life after death, God or heaven and hell, we are not taking our mansions with us. All of our property and material belongings will remain here. Others will inherit and share our creations or materials things whether we like it or not.

We do not need to "own" anything. Ownership of property,

buildings, cars, money or commodities is not natural to our true state of being, nor is it natural to this realm of existence, which is ever changing and evolving. Even though there may temporary satisfaction in having material things, humans are only stewards of the material world. When we fix ourselves to something in the attempt to "own" it, we are actually stunting our spiritual growth. We are blocking the evolvement of our souls. The historical study of evolved spiritual figures is proof of this. Spiritual leaders such as Gandhi, Jesus or Mother Theresa never desired to acquire money, property or materials things. They found happiness and peace in owning nothing—yet they had everything. On the other hand, leaders such as Hitler, Caesar, or J. P. Morgan attempted to own, control and amass as much as they could and found only misery. The more a person attempts to own the material world, the more the soul of that person shuts down and spiritual growth comes to a standstill. There are a few souls alive today who are living examples of this lesson; the realization that great personal wealth leads to a spiritual dead end. After amassing great wealth, these few souls are giving back to humanity.

Again, we do not need to "own" anything—not even our home or place of residence. With the new economic values of United Credit, it is possible to have all that you need or all that you desire to fulfill your life purpose without "debt" or mortgages. Every living person on this planet has a right to a home. Shelter is a basic human need and home ownership is one of those basic needs that has been exploited terribly by capitalism. (The idea of the right to have a home without worrying about debt or a mortgage will be developed further in the following chapters.)

The resources to provide every person with a home are available. However, these resources are drastically out of balance. Someone is living in a 50-room mansion while owning 5 other homes around the world. On the other end, someone is living in a cardboard shack on the edge of a dump. Can you imagine hoarding millions of dollars in a bank account while two billion people in this world are so poor that they cannot afford basic shelter? Can you imagine building a garage for multiple fancy sport cars when one hundred million people in this world are homeless? I find these actions to be unthinkable.

The greed often fueling the social economy in America is out of control. An example of this is our automobile industry. Just after the great Wall Street bailout, our government initiated a "cash for clunkers" economic incentive program. Americans were encouraged to trade perfectly good cars for new ones—vehicles that got better gas mileage. Most of the vehicles that were traded in were crushed, even though many of them were decent used vehicles. The whole program did nothing but prop up a dying automobile industry by creating a little more demand in a market that is already over saturated and on its last leg. Few of the traded in vehicles were donated to individuals, families or organizations in need. Greed was working on both ends and it seemed as if nobody cared at all. If an organization such as United Credit had been in existence, all of those cars could have been acquired and then distributed to people who needed them—people who were giving their time and energy to help others.

Money is always a means to something else. It is nothing of **real** value. In reality, our money has evolved into nothing but dirty paper. Yet, we have built a whole economy and credit system based on it. What would happen if we built an economy based on helping each other and on doing meaningful things; a currency based on the exchange of human energy? Somehow, we have to build a bridge from a dying and valueless economic system to a thriving and meaningful economic system.

Eventually, I am going to die and pass over to the next realm. It is interesting that most people in our society conform to the concept of having their "affairs" in order for when they die. Why do we have to die to have our affairs in order? Why can't we share what we have while we are alive? Most of us are missing the boat. Our purpose here on this planet is to be good stewards of the material world. By helping those in need, and by distributing the wealth I acquire while I am alive, I can free myself from the perils of material attachments. In the end, everything that we own and have created is passed on to others.

We must remember that all that we create in terms of the material world is nothing of real value or meaning and nothing that will last in the march of time. What will last are the deeds —the human creations and accomplishments of the mind, heart and soul. What is remembered is not the fancy car or the big house. What is remembered is the way a person lives—the compassion, kindness, leadership and understanding that the person exemplified!

COMMUNISM? SOCIALISM? HUMANISM!

One of the most basic obstacles to any type of new economic philosophy will be how it is labeled politically. Thus, I feel it is very important to address this matter right from the start.

The philosophy of economics is still in its infancy stage. Humanity is adrift on an economic raft that is leaking and slowly sinking. From the beginning of this era of trade, commerce and money, there has never been a meaningful economic philosophy based on the real needs of people. All of our economic philosophies have more or less evolved out of social/economic failure, revolution, rationalism or the immediate need to understand a process already in motion. **The acquisition of material wealth, money and the ownership of land and property has been the process in motion from the beginning of Western history.**

By far, the economic system that now dominates most all world societies is capitalism. Capitalism evolved from economic activity focused on accumulation of wealth (greed). Whether this accumulation of wealth was amassed by individuals, kings, religious institutions or governments, it has been by far the most common economic activity in historical and modern times. All other economic philosophies or systems, such as socialism or communism evolved out of the struggles against the growing beast of capitalism. Mainstream economists today predominantly rely on classical rationalism (pure reason or valueless social science) as they develop their theories and economic systems. Thus, at the root of all economic philosophy today, there is no spiritual, moral or ethical foundation.

The word "economy" comes from the Greek work *oikos* meaning "neighborhood" and *nomos* meaning "law" and "order". The word "economy" originated from the need to create order to the emerging world of trade and commerce. What was lost in the centuries that followed and in the whole realm of economic philosophy was the real purpose of "economy". The purpose of the social economy was not meant to increase the accumulation of wealth or to rationalize corporate greed. The true purpose of the social economy was meant to satisfy the needs of families and to promote the spiritual welfare and happiness of people.

One does not have to study world history very long before realizing that the wealth and material power has been most often concentrated in the hands of a few, while the masses struggled to fulfill their basic human needs. By the 15th and 16th centuries and just before the industrial revolution, religious and political monarchies controlled most of the wealth in the Western world. In many cases, it was the same in the Eastern world. Once the industrial revolution began, the ability to accumulate and acquire wealth by the select few became greatly enhanced while the plight of the masses (working class) headed down the road of greater despair. By the end of the 19th century, serious class struggles arose and modern socialism developed.

Socialism, at its beginning, was essentially a working class political movement that attempted to create more material equality in society. It was an attempt to take the concentrated wealth and material power out of the hands of a few and redistribute it among the masses—the working classes. Socialism can justifiably be called a reactionary economic philosophy. The social revolutions that followed the "socialist" philosophers were certainly with good cause but never with a truly humanitarian economic philosophy on which to build new societies. A perfect example is the 1918 socialist revolution in Germany, which deposed the monarchy. We all know what eventually evolved by the late 1930's as the means of production as well as the produced assets ended up being controlled and managed by a centralized bureaucracy.

Communism is really an extension of socialism, which like socialism, was not founded on a sound economic philosophy. Communism evolved as a radical rejection of imperialist and capitalist societies. As a branch of socialism, communism was thought by some to be the final stage in human society: a classless, stateless society based on common and equal ownership of not only the means of production, but all that is produced. It sounds good on paper, but to this day there has never been one *pure* social example of communism. Whether it be China, Russia or North Korea—whether it be Marxism, Leninism, Maoism or the different aspects of Eurocommunism—all communist social attempts have been fraught with dictatorships; and in more recent years, oligarchies (leaders concerned not with the common good, but with increasing personal wealth and property ownership/control as much as possible). Of course the most obvious failure of communism is that it never took into account the spiritual needs of human beings.

As mentioned above, the true purpose of the social economy was meant to satisfy the needs of families and to promote the spiritual welfare and happiness of people. Current economic theories or economic "sciences" such as Neoclassical, Keynesian, Trickle Down, Mutualism, etc. are all void of this basic economic philosophy and are often attempts to define, understand or promote capitalist/corporate economic activity. These rational economic sciences embrace greed, self-interest and corporate freedom as having the potential to create positive social outcomes. Obviously, the opposite has happened. Corporate freedom has led to less freedom and prosperity for the majority of the world's people.

The bottom line is this: how does a society manage their external/material goods while attending to the human needs of all its individuals? How do you manage or equate fairness to services and labor verses food, housing, education, art, music and all the basic human needs of the individual or family? How do you prevent a system of economics that allows market investment and speculation, hedge funding and all the types of capitalist schemes that can quickly transfer collective social wealth into the hands of a few? These are the issues of today. These are the issues that must be addressed at this current moment in human history. Without a real economic philosophy and new economic system, the world will likely continue to fall into economic chaos. We may have a few short spurts of grow and reprieve, but, as stated earlier, capitalism has its own end in sight.

What is proposed in this book (the philosophy of United Credit) does not fall into any of the above-mentioned economic systems. What is proposed is a new economic philosophy based on the real **human** needs and actions of all people. We need an economic philosophy that begins with humanitarian principles and ethics. We need an economic system that begins with human actions and deeds that are dedicated to alleviating the suffering of others—an economic system that is built on a truly moral, ethical and humanitarian base.

A truly humanitarian based economic philosophy or system has to begin with taking care of both the material and spiritual needs of individuals and their communities. It has to also be developed to deal with the larger social and worldly economic, political and environmental issues. Can a new economic system evolve out of the current economic system, or will it only be able to evolve out of the ashes of capitalism? That is the question. I write this book in hopes that a bridge can be built between the present and the future world economies. Considering that America's dollar has no real value (only believed value), it is imperative that a new economic model based on real value begins to emerge.

An economic model such as United Credit could potentially evolve into a new form of trade and commerce as well as take on some of the most important humanitarian issues of today such as food, housing, education and energy. United Credit, from the start, would have to be created and maintained with a whole new and innovative set of organizational/humanitarian guidelines. Such an organization would need checks and balances to promote fair, balanced and honest distribution of all resources needed by human beings to live healthy and happy lives. United Credit would need to be created with checks and balances to prevent greed, individual profit and political corruption.

We must go back to our economic roots and create (for the first time in human history) a truly humanitarian economic philosophy. As stated earlier, the purpose of the social economy is not meant to increase the accumulation of individual wealth. The true purpose of the social economy is meant to satisfy the basic needs of individuals, families and communities in order to promote the spiritual welfare and happiness of all people.

When creating new models of social economy, the issues of ownership will need to be addressed in ways that insure equality and fairness. We will have to go beyond socialist ideas into a realm of humanitarian principles. We will have to transform our concepts of economy to incorporate a worldview —one that is always focused on the advancement of humanity and the preservation of the delicate ecosphere in which we live.

The rest of this book is an attempt to lay some foundational stones for this process.

Part 2

United Credit and the Foundations of Economic Reform

Creating an Economic Constitution

In order to foster new economic philosophy based on humanitarian values, it will be necessary to create an economic constitution—a set of humanitarian codes to guide societies into a new golden age of compassion, sharing and economic equality. We must create an economic constitution that can and will be embraced on a global level and that perhaps will someday be instituted by a Global Economic Congress. This is the time for humanity to act. In our rapidly changing technological world, all of the boundaries between countries, cultures and individuals are vanishing. It is imperative that a worldview be taken by any new economic philosophy or a new set of economic codes. It is also imperative that any new economic worldview take into consideration the social/economic needs of poor countries. It is also imperative that new economic world views take into consideration environmental protection and sustainability. No longer can we accept the economic dictation and imperialistic policies of the rich countries and private corporations.

All around the globe, people are demanding new economic principles, values and institutions that promote equality and fairness.

Unfortunately, humanity will need laws to implement an economic constitution. Greed has been implanted in our souls. Capitalism has tainted our genetic framework. In order to implement a new economic philosophy, whether nationally or globally, there will need to be a couple of generations guided by a well written and well enforced economic constitution. There will also have to be a new set of penal codes incorporated into a new economic constitution—penalties designed to reform the human heart and soul—**not to punish**. This is an important point in going forward with a new economic philosophy. Human beings have been conditioned in recent generations by capitalism and concepts of greed and acquisition. Old habits will die hard and people cannot be punished for deeds coming from past conditioning. People can and must be reformed. Human values must be transformed. Change can and will begin in the human heart.

The first step in creating an economic constitution is to establish a new philosophy with basic economic principles that honor human existence on this planet—principles that not only honor our present existence, but also the future existence of humanity. This can be accomplished by creating an economic bill of rights that hopefully would lead to an International Economic Congress (IEC).

Unlike the current global economic institutions like the World Bank, the International Monetary Fund and the World Trade Organization, an International Economic Congress would **work against** economic policies that benefit rich corporations, as well as trade organizations that force developing Nations into cycles of ever increasing debt. The current economic policies of organizations like the World Bank have brought many societies to the brink of major economic upheaval; providing billions of dollars in loans to developing countries—loans that have been designed to subsidize global corporations to gain control over emerging economies as well as their natural resources. The examples of these types of economic policies are far too many. Creating a new economic organization to help countries manage diverse economies, natural resources, fair trade, labor rights and environmental issues will be critically important in coming years.

There are currently many truly humanitarian people working all over the world for various causes. Electing the right individuals to form an International Economic Congress would not be a challenging issue. As far as creating an economic bill of rights, I think the basics are self-evident:

Right number one:

All people have a right to share in the fruit of the planet —food. No inequalities in food stocks and supplies should be allowed in this age of globalism. All individual, national and international hunger issues should be addressed as first priority by all people and more importantly by a potential organization such as an International Economic Congress (IEC). Redistribution of food supplies and stocks should and would be a first and foremost priority. No longer would first world economies be allowed to support "all you can eat" buffets and food splurging establishments. No longer would corporations be allowed to control food resources for greed and profit. Corporations that practice in the manipulation of seeds, fertilizers, farmland, etc. would have to be brought under control. Corporations that attempt to control food supplies would have to develop humanitarian guidelines in order to continue operating. Governments that are currently paying farm subsidies for farmers not to grow crops would have to shift towards paying farmers to return to sustainable farming practices.

Right number two:

All people have a right to a reasonably comfortable and safe home. Any and all material resources to build and create homes for all humans on this planet should be shared globally. An organization such as an International Economic Congress could potentially manage the implementation of this right. On a community or national level, United Credit could supply the resources to sustain this right. No longer should individuals be allowed to own more than one home when there are others without a home. No longer should individuals be allowed to build a 50-room mansion when others are living in cardboard shacks. Homes that are foreclosed upon and sitting empty should have to be turned over to a foundation such as United Credit to be redistributed to those working towards a better life and a humanitarian world! No longer should lending or trading institutions be allowed to "bundle" and sell the titles to homes. The IEC could implement laws to ensure that, eventually, all existing and new homes in the world would be co-operatively owned and shared from generation to generation.

As mentioned in an earlier chapter, there is no need to own anything in this ever changing and temporary world—homes are meant to be shared, and eventually passed on. This may seem as a very radical proposal, but it's really one of the basic building blocks to solving the world economic crisis today, as later chapters will reveal.

Right number three:

All people have a right to basic healthcare. Corporate greed and profit in all healthcare systems will have to be eradicated, and eventually become a crime punishable by human service work for months or years depending on the need of reform. A global system of sharing healthcare professionals, healthcare technology and resources could be easily implemented by the IEC. The whole concept of profit—whether it be pharmaceutical corporations, hospitals, medical suppliers or insurance companies—is ridiculous. There is no ethical or moral foundation behind these commercial institutions. The bottom line is this: it is not ethical or morally right to profit from the illness of others. Once an expanded spiritual and moral philosophy is injected into the whole concept of healthcare, humanity will someday look back to our current age as one of barbarianism!

Right number four:

All people have a right to education. If there were equality with food, housing and healthcare, why would humans need to pay for education? The IEC and United Credit would guarantee free education to all people.

Right number five:

All humans should have access to the humanities—art, music, literature, theater, etc. The failure of political and economic systems to provide this right has resulted in the rise of neglect, crime, depression and negativity on the planet. Right now there are 12 year-old children working 60-70 hours a week in overseas corporate sweat shops sewing the clothes that line the racks of Walmart, JC Penney and all other US and European chain stores. These children yearn for art and music just as we all do. What gives anyone the right to enslave another soul? What gives anyone the right to deny the beauty, happiness and spiritual development of a child? Are the corporations building educational institutions for these third world children? I don't think so. The basic right to the humanities is critical to creating a new economic philosophy. People who are happy are healthier, wiser and more willing to help others. Art, music and theater can inspire us to look outside of our own needs and wants.

Right number six:

All human beings have a right to the world's energy resources. It is immoral and unethical for people to profit from the resources of this planet, which are here for all people to share. More importantly, humans have the right to free energy. The knowledge and technology to provide free/clean energy sources have been developed and are available. There are many new advances in this field waiting to be funded and put into practical applications in all aspects of social economy. Capitalism has continually repressed and stunted energy technology—something that must end. This economic right—the right to free/clean energy—is the most critical right of all, considering the state of affairs on this planet and the destruction of our environment. United Credit can and will have a great part in creating a new foundation for change in this arena as will be discussed later in this section.

Right number seven:

All human beings have a right to clean water, clean oceans, un-polluted environments and non-toxic air. Humanity is faced with some very severe environmental issues in the coming years. All people should have a choice in the direction taken by governments and corporations in the areas of environmental protection.

These are seven basic economic rights to which all people should be entitled; each right would have its bill of sub-rights. It is critical that the groundwork for a new economic constitution be put in place now. Our current economic system is failing and there will be a huge economic vacuum in the near future needing to be filled. If this vacuum is not filled, we will experience a long period of global chaos filled with vagabonds, warlords, homelessness, slavery and worst things we can only imagine. A new economic constitution must be put in place before a global economic collapse!

The American Constitution is an amazing document. It was a major breakthrough for humanity and for the rights of individuals. But it's not all written. It is not complete and it will never be complete until there is a basic bill of *economic rights* incorporated into it. I believe that the American Constitution can be used as a framework for a new International/World constitution that not only addresses economic rights but all basic human rights as well. Until all world leaders accept the fact that there will be no peace or true prosperity until a truly humanitarian global bill of basic economic rights is adopted, the human drama will continue to slip into a very dark and dismal age—one that I do not wish on anyone, myself or my children.

UNITED CREDIT AND FOOD RESOURCES
(Right Number 1)

The foundations for equality in food distribution on this planet are already in place. There are many humanitarian organizations already working diligently to put an end to world hunger. However, it is never enough. There are millions of children in our own country—America—who go to bed hungry every night. I can foresee United Credit becoming a core foundation in the area of food distribution and equality. Once the United Credit foundation is established, funded and supported, credit will need to be extended to all humanitarian organizations that are currently working to redistribute food resources. Most importantly, United Credit would work with communities to find long-term solutions for agricultural sustainability.

Remember—In moving from an economic system based on money to an era of prosperity without money, United Credit will need to be funded, supported and created with money and material resources in the beginning! Ultimately, as new economic values evolve, United Credit would be able to dissolve money and remove it from the economy. As radical as this might sound, it is the only way towards the ultimate survival of humanity as time will prove.

Secondly, United Credit would have to work with food corporations and farmers on a large scale. There are horrible things happening in America's food supply chain these days. It is overwhelming to even imagine that certain corporations are genetically altering seeds, such as soy and corn that form the basic blocks of our food. This genetic altering has enabled crops to withstand toxic pesticides. The end result at this time is that Americans, and increasingly more people world-wide are eating genetically altered, pesticide tainted food. Worse than this, farmers are being forced into this method of food production all across this country and certain corporations are currently pushing the American Congress to pass detrimental laws regarding farming and food production in order to gain more capitalistic control (the "Food Safety" bill S.510 for example—a bill that could eventually suppress organic farming) .

Obviously, this is a major issue and will have to be addressed by humanity on a large scale at some point in the future. United Credit, however, could address this issue in small and important ways right now. Extending credit to organic farms, natural seed suppliers and supporting community gardens would be a powerful start to a major grass-roots method of change. Imagine the possibilities this opens up in the early days of the United Credit Foundation! Imagine all the opportunities for people in need to earn United credit while working to grow healthy food in community gardens, saving natural seeds for future gardens, or helping to distribute the food. I can envision natural farms where people have the opportunity to not only give their time and effort, but to recreate their whole lives.

Once a foundation such as United Credit is in place, many potential opportunities for people who are in need would begin to manifest. How many food banks are there across this country that are in need of assistance? How many of these food banks would welcome fresh, locally grown organic food? With difficult economic times on the horizon, it is critical that communities develop methods of providing food for their members—not just in this country, but around the world. An economic collapse could potentially shut down corporate farming and food distribution. This is one of the most important issues of our time: how are we going to feed ourselves, now that whole generations have been raised on grocery store inventories rather than homesteads and farms?

Innovations in organic food production and clean water supplies must also be promoted and supported—winter greenhouses, hydroponics and small home winter garden kits and water purification systems for example. There are whole industries that an organization like United Credit could foster immediately and that could prosper without any exchange of money.

On the larger scale, businesses and corporations could be solicited to join the foundation in some meaningful way. A world food bank could be created in the near future and donations to such a food bank could be rewarded with credit from the foundation—this credit not being compensated with money, but with human resources. United Credit could offer endless opportunities for people in need of work within an organized world food bank.

The current practices of converting food sources such as corn into ethanol fuel products need to be halted. There are far more efficient ways to create fuel/energy without using the world's precious and limited food supplies. United Credit would need to work hard to help shift energy/fuel technologies away from food sources by fully supporting and extending credit to companies that pursue alternative, clean and renewable fuel sources.

FOOD is the most important issue of humanity. Americans may not feel the pressure of dwindling food resources, but much of the developing world feels this pressure first hand and it is getting worse by the month. Americans need to deal with this issue now, and more importantly, Americans need to deal with the fact that much of our food is poisoned, genetically altered and full of harmful additives—all for the massive profits of a few greedy corporations. Just look around at all the cancer and obesity in America. Our meat and dairy is full of growth hormones and antibiotics. Of course this is affecting our population. What are the future health problems from these new genetically altered seeds, livestock feed, corn, soy, etc.? Now these greedy corporations have openly announced that they want to control all vegetable seeds within two years and make it a criminal offense for the average small farm to grow organically. Can you imagine such a corporate dominated society? Well, it is here and now we are going to have to deal with it. United Credit would make it a priority to deal with this issue.

UNITED CREDIT AND HOUSING
(Right number 2)

In my mind, the solution to the American (and world) housing crises is a no-brainer. Before getting into potential solutions however, let's look a little closer at the problem. How did we get so deep into immoral and unethical home financing, real-estate valuations and the trading of home securities? The answer: CAPITALISM!

You know, it was not that long ago when communities used to come together and build a newlywed couple or a needy family a new home. This home was freely given and there were no greedy strings attached, no variable rate mortgages! Eventually, these homes were passed on to surviving family members or community groups. It was simple and pure. There are still places in this world where this method of housing creation is still practiced, but greed has been spreading rapidly by luring humans into the conceptual framework of debt and worry regarding their basic right to live and have a home.

As stated earlier in the book, there is no earthly reason why anyone has to own land or own a home. Homes should be communal property with rights given to individuals and families, as their needs and circumstances change. United Credit could immediately help resolve the housing crises in America by acquiring as many foreclosed homes as possible and establishing a housing bank. Individuals and families in need of a home who are willing to give their time and energy in whatever ways they could to help others would be granted a home (mortgage free). Of course, the first thing the skeptics will say is that people will not appreciate or take care of something given to them, but I feel that this would not be the case. The whole basis of United Credit is about creating self-worth and self-esteem. No one is getting anything for free. Everyone, however, is getting an opportunity to change and better their lives—opportunities that have not been available to this degree in our modern society.

As of January 2011, there were approximately 18.4 million homes sitting empty in the United States. These properties were being held by the large banks, some of which have already received billions in Government bailout money. Rather than auction them off at market value to people who may be able to afford them, these banks are holding them hoping that the Government will eventually bail them out again and buy them at book value, which is currently higher than market value. Americans are being held hostage by the lending institutions! This is a crime against society and a crime against every hard working American. Where is the real social economy—the one that is meant to promote the health and happiness of its people? Over eighteen million homes are sitting empty because a few greedy barons want to continue to profit and get bailed out—this after committing mortgage fraud on an unprecedented scale!

Imagine if all 18.4 million homes currently sitting empty were acquired by United Credit and were redistributed as needed to those helping others. The shift in social/economic consciousness that needs to happen is that no person's home should ever have to be viewed or used as an asset to increase the wealth of others. The value of a home should be measured by the stability, peace and happiness it brings to the persons or families occupying it. That value should never be compromised and it should be transferred to others promoting a healthy and happy social economy.

As I write this chapter, there is another 2.5 million more

homes expected to fall into foreclosure in 2012. A possible solution to such a home foreclosure crisis could be provided by an organization such as United Credit. Homeowners could be given the option to turn over their homes to the United Credit housing bank with the security of being able to stay in their home indefinitely and mortgage free! Of course, an important part of this arrangement would be the home owner's willingness to be a part of the United Credit foundation—helping others in whatever ways they could. United Credit would assume all repairs and maintenance of their property, and the homeowner would have the comfort and assurance of knowing that their home would be gratefully taken over by others in need when they no longer lived in it. It is important to give people who are in trouble with their home mortgages an opportunity to really save their home. Give people the opportunity to remove their home from the dockets of greedy, home-stealing banks and they will grasp that opportunity.

One major problem to this solution is that so many people have been trapped by the current economic system into using their homes as a form of wealth building—retirement assets, loan equity, etc. As we are seeing now, these aspects of home ownership are shifting as home values decrease. The "wealth building" aspects of home ownership have only served to build the wealth of a few and have allowed the Federal Reserve and large banks to get a greater strangle hold on American people. It's time for society to re-evaluate home values and realize that any home is only worth the comfort, security and happiness it brings to the persons occupying it!

Of course, all the many other aspects of United Credit fall into place in terms of taking care of a large housing bank—connecting the plumber who needs food for his family to the house that needs someone to install a new furnace—the nurse who needs a home to the elderly person who needs special home care..... I could go on with examples, but all the relations set in motion by helping others—by giving people the real opportunity to help others which in turn betters the lives of those giving of themselves. This becomes an endless potential of chain reactions. Finding real and meaningful solutions to put families back into empty homes would be a powerful step towards creating a real economy, rather than continuing to prop up the current artificial economy.

On the larger scale, United Credit could begin to acquire resources—materials and skilled people to help communities in other parts of the world create housing for those in need. I have to insert here that what I see happening in the years following the 2010 earthquake in Haiti is shameful in terms of the global community. At last count, there were over 100,000 people still living in tent camps almost a year later. What has gone wrong on this planet? Is this the pattern of future human reaction when masses of people lose their homes by way of major calamities? Is it possible that there is no world organization capable of dealing with such mass calamities and large-scale loss of housing? If that is the case, something needs to be done now. Our Earth is changing fast due to the removal of coal, oil, natural gas and other resources from the planet's crustal mass. More intense natural disasters are surely in our future.

Putting calamities aside, there are millions of people on this planet right now in need of a home. Building resources have been drastically mismanaged from country to county and within countries. As mentioned earlier, where is the moral justification for an individual building a garage to house fancy sport cars while others are living without even the basic of shelters? Where is the moral justification for the corporate hospitality industry building larger and more lavish resorts and hotels in areas where they end up overshadowing extreme poverty? Besides acquiring building materials and other resources, United Credit could build a collection of skilled trades people who are willing and able to build homes for others. There are a few organizations already moving into this humanitarian mode and these organizations could be supported by United Credit. Excessive building practices will have to be challenged. The concept of owning multiple homes will have to be challenged. Imagine how many potential homes could be donated to United Credit once such a new economic model starts to take hold.

Already, a link between economic rights 1 and 2 develops; United Credit could acquire a large farm that needs renovation. People are then given opportunities on many levels to help renovate, to plant and grow food, thus being able to live in a stress free and peaceful home environment. How many people out there are homeless in this country alone who are in need of such opportunities? These opportunities can promote happiness, health and productivity—all without the need for, or the exchange of money.

Another very important area of the housing market that could be addressed by an organization such as United Credit is the developing industry of *Zero Energy* home construction. The knowledge, technology and products to create *Zero Energy* homes (no fossil fuel dependency) is real and a budding industry. These *Zero Energy* homes only need to be outfitted with solar and other alternative energies to run appliances, heating and lights. There is no reason to continue building homes dependent on dinosaur remains (fossil fuels). Humanity is stuck in the muck of oil, tar and gas! United Credit would be in the forefront of supporting the *Zero Energy* industry. Imagine the new opportunities and jobs that would be created!

In the bigger picture, I can see the foundation of United Credit helping to build whole new communities of people working together building *Zero Energy* homes that are gifted to families mortgage free. I can see United Credit soliciting the large monopolizing corporations to donate to the foundation or risk being listed as non-humanitarian companies and boycotted. A simple shift in our values regarding homes and housing could start a wave of humanitarian change.

UNITED CREDIT AND HEALTHCARE
(Right number 3)

There is no better example of economic failure in this country, or for that matter in the world, than the American healthcare system. Capitalism has created an ugly, selfish and immoral beast. As I was writing this chapter, our Senators and Congressional leaders were hog-boggling over whether how and why all Americans should have the right to basic healthcare. They were doing this while they themselves, were privileged to the best gold plated healthcare plans money can buy.

It is a fact that in 2010, 50 to 60 million Americans had no health insurance. Another 25 million or more were quickly falling into the healthcare abyss, as their rates were climbing out of reach or they were becoming drastically uninsured. America is the only industrialized country in the world that does not have universal healthcare. In all areas of healthcare ranking such as infant mortality, life expectancy, immunization and preventable diseases, America ranks 20th or worse. America's healthcare costs are 40 to 50% higher than any other industrialized nation, yet we are providing less and less coverage to our citizens with the highest rates for healthcare expenditures.

According to T.R Reed—one of the leading researchers regarding world healthcare systems:

"The United States is the only developed country that relies on profit-making healthcare insurance companies to pay for essential and elective care....but a significant share of the premium dollar goes to cover the costs of marketing, underwriting and administration as well their **profit**. Economists agree that this is about the most expensive possible way to pay for a nation's health care..."

Mr. Reed continues:

"How many people go bankrupt because of medical bills? In France, zero. In Japan, Germany, the Netherlands, Canada and Switzerland, zero. In the United States, according to a joint study in 2005 by the Harvard Law School and the Harvard Medical School, the annual figure is around 700,000. ...."

And:

"American health insurance also differs from the other countries on the question of "guaranteed issue." In other developed countries, health insurance plans are required by LAW to guarantee coverage for anybody. American insurance firms, though, are allowed to pick and choose their customers and avoid the wrong ones. They pour large sums of money into efforts to cherry-pick the right customers and avoid the wrong ones. That way, they can avoid selling health insurance to the people who need the most health care—and are the most expensive to cover. The United States is the only developed country that allows insurance companies to refuse coverage to people for fear that they might get sick."

(T.R. Reed—*The Healing of America*)

Our current healthcare system has been built on the same valueless economic foundation that everything else in our society has been built on: capitalism. There is no hope for any and all healthcare plans being debated or passed by our congress that continue to support capitalistic economic models. They will fail. The wealthy drug corporations, the massive, greedy insurance corporations, and many other special interest groups are spending millions of dollars to lobby our congress people in order to prevent a move towards any type of universal healthcare.

Let me ask for a moment: How would senators and congress people justify the recent situation of a young Colorado fire-fighter who spent the last few summers fighting forest fires throughout the west and now has been diagnosed with cancer—a public service worker who has been risking his life for $20,000 a year? His first round of diagnostic testing was $16,000 alone. He has no insurance. He was provided no insurance. His meager income was just over the limit for State Medicare insurance. I could list thousands of examples like this currently playing out across America. Something is seriously wrong with our society to ever allow such situations to exist.

I could go into pages and pages of information about our failing healthcare system but I think it's clear that there is no better place to begin to implement a new economic model—a new economic philosophy—than our healthcare system. Call it United Credit; call it whatever you want....we need a new economic philosophy. We need to infuse a whole new value system into our healthcare system from the bottom up and from the top down—not-for-profit healthcare. We need to create a bridge from what we have now to something meaningful, lasting and successful. United Credit offers that hope—that change our healthcare system so badly needs and that all people deserve.

Where do we begin?

We must create an organization such as United Credit. We must create a humanitarian foundation based on a new economic model. We must define the immediate needs of both the healthcare system and the society it serves and work in order to transform them.

There are 50 million people in this country with no

healthcare, and likely there will still be that many with no healthcare after current government programs are passed (if they are passed and instituted). Most of the 50 million people without healthcare are already living on the edge and will not be able to "buy-in" for any percentage of their income. Many of the uninsured are children, chronically ill or elderly, perhaps, but most are average working people—average mothers and fathers. Why can't we give these people an opportunity to earn their healthcare by giving some of their time and effort to provide for the basic needs of the healthcare industry itself? Millions of Americans have been self-employed their whole lives. They cannot afford healthcare and often would refuse to receive any type of welfare, even if they qualified for it. However, if given the chance, many of them would gladly give 20 hours or more per month helping to transport patients or family members back and forth to the hospital, provide grounds keeping, or whatever other community service they could do in exchange for basic health care. If I was given this type of opportunity, I would be proud and happy to know that I was giving something of myself—a meaningful service to others in exchange for a service that I may need someday. The benefit for the hospital or healthcare facility from people giving their time and energy is money saved. Money saved goes back into the system to be given to others in need.

The United Credit Foundation would not only work to establish databases of healthcare facilities and other social organizations in need of donated services, they would also begin to set up special clinics managed and run by clinically trained individuals who desire to give 20 or more hours a month to help those in need. People can be inspired to come into the system with the desire to be part of a new healthcare model on both ends: giving and receiving. I do not think there are too many doctors or nurses out there that would turn away from being part of a program where needy, uninsured Americans are attempting to give of their time and energy to help others—Americans who are willing to earn the healthcare that they deserve.

I have to stop for a moment here and say that it is very tragic that the healthcare system of our country has come to the point that the basic right of healthcare—**any type of medical care**—can be denied. It is tragic that I am even sitting here attempting to write this chapter. You can bet that even the most "primitive" tribes of antiquity took care of their sick and needy. They did this without the expectation of gain or acquisition. You can bet that the old medicine woman might have taken some meat or a hide as payment or trade for her herbs, but never would she have demanded it. She would have given freely to her people! In ancient China, doctors were only paid when people were healthy because their system focused on preventative care. Somewhere along the road of capitalistic expansion, our society lost its sense of connectedness and humanity. Now the question is: how do we get it back?

If all people should have a right to basic healthcare, then the whole idea of people having to earn healthcare credit by serving others is really quite a paradox! The real issue here is developing a new value system—a re-education of our thinking. Healthcare needs, like many other human needs, should not be taken advantage of for profit—not by insurance companies—medical corporations, or by anyone. Most of all, the best of healthcare or any type of human need technology and services should not be reserved for the "wealthy" class of society. The whole purpose of United Credit from day one would be to create an increasingly equal access channel for all to fulfill their basic human needs including their medical needs. People should be able to do this without being forced into debt or homelessness.

This is not an unattainable goal. France (rated the best health care system in the world by the World Health Organization) provides equal access healthcare to all its citizens with privately run medical facilities (not socialism) and they do this at less than one third the cost of our healthcare system in America.

If you are poor or homeless in America, you have virtually no healthcare other than the worst emergency situations of life and death (if you are lucky). The truth is that the poor and the homeless have the most serious healthcare needs. They often feel helpless and lost—rejected by society. However, all people deserve basic healthcare. Who are we as Americans to judge or dish out selective healthcare services? In reality, the poor and the homeless people can be given a new and exciting opportunity to come back into the social system—a system that would be on the brink of revolutionary changes in values and human care. Let's use a case in point—a worst case scenario:

I once had a friend who was drafted into the Army and sent to Vietnam. He was a tall, handsome and talented Native American. One of his talents was art and painting. He was an amazing portrait artist. For the sake of this book, I'll call him Robert. Robert was a sharp person and a fast learner. He was quickly moved into Army flight school and was trained as a helicopter pilot. His assignments involved dropping napalm on jungle villages. After each successful drop, he celebrated at the officer's club, laughed and joked with the other pilots.

Then, in an instant, Robert's whole reality changed forever. During one of his next drop missions, his helicopter was shot down after dumping its napalm load. Robert and the other crew members survived the crash and immediately became witnesses to the insidious act they had just perpetrated on a sleepy jungle village. Woman and children were running in every direction literally burning alive. Robert snapped that day —soon to be discharged from the army for "mental disability".

Needless to say, society gave Robert a very unwelcome homecoming. He was unable to cope with life or integrate back into society. He was in pain and used alcohol all the time to escape the horrible, recurring nightmares and flashbacks. He ended up homeless and distraught. Despite the few social/ personal attempts by society to help Robert, there was no system in place to help Robert integrate back into society.... to feel useful and to heal and recover from his tragic war experience. This scenario is being recreated all over again for thousands of young men and women. In five or ten years, how many of these mentally and/or physically wounded Veterans coming back from the Middle East will end up homeless on America's streets? As it stands today, there are thousands of Vietnam vets homeless.

In a different, future reality United Credit, already having built its foundation, would have trained persons ready and willing to donate their time on the streets helping the homeless with basic needs. Once identified, individual Veterans could be offered, and perhaps directed to special programs depending on their particular abilities. For example, Veterans might be able to relate to the wounded servicemen and woman coming back from Afghanistan. My friend Robert was an amazing portrait artist. He could have been offered a job visiting and accompanying wounded Vets while drawing their portraits for family members. He loved to draw and paint, but in the early years after his return, no one took him seriously even though his skill level was on the level of a master painter.

Both of America's healthcare and mental care institutions have missed the boat. Taking care of ordinary Americans, or homeless war Veterans is not about the lack of money (in the case of the Veteran's Administration) or making money! There are so many creative ways to revolutionize our value system right now!

Perhaps in Robert's case, some sort of treatment, counseling or guidance program would be needed. Starting from the top down implies finding those skilled persons willing to be a part of the United Credit foundation. In exchange for their time and energies, they too would receive credit from the foundation—credit that could be used to help with their needs. The important key to creating a successful foundation is to quickly evolve the credit reward aspect of the foundation.

Imagine someone like Robert, once enrolled in the system, he finds and embraces a rewarding opportunity to share his talents. Perhaps he heals some of his wounds and desires to improve his life. United Credit, already having acquired homes out of the foreclosure processes happening all over this country, gives Robert a small cozy home and helps set him up to manage it. This could and would have to be done without strapping Robert with a rent payment or mortgage! As long as Robert is giving into the system in the ways that he is able to, there is no need for United Credit or anyone else to profit from his place of residence. Robert deserves a decent, peaceful place to live in with honor for serving his country! After all, he fought for our country so that the rest of us could have a peaceful place to live.

Unfortunately, Robert is no longer with us. He was abandoned by our society and left to fend for himself. He ultimately drank himself to death. The fact that he was Native American did not help him while waiting for the Veteran's Administration to come through. My point here is clear. Currently, there is no system available in our country, other than welfare that people in emergency need can turn to in order to better their lives, while keeping and building dignity. Without dignity, we breed failure, depression and dependence.

We are dealing with a healthcare system that is grasping for profit and forgetting about the real needs of both the patients and the providers! We are dealing with a system that is destroying the souls of the people who depend on it! We have to institute a whole new value system based on giving and helping each other! Can you imagine what it is like for that uninsured waitress who has to bring her daughter to the emergency room with a serious illness and gets a bill for $4,500 two weeks later, and then has no money to pay the bill? How would that make you feel? Would it hurt your pride or dignity? It would hurt mine and it would also make me angry. If we lived in Cuba, such a scenario would and could not happen. You can say what you want about Castro but he got it right with social healthcare!

Another case in point: Let me go back to the California couple who lost their jobs at the hospital where they worked. They ended up killing their children and committing suicide. This type of tragic incident should have never happened. It's insane that it did. Other than unemployment or welfare, what system was in place to help this couple with their immediate needs? Considering this country has a healthcare institution that is so full of holes, gaps and in need of dedicated people—how did this couple fall through the cracks? Hospitals and other medical institutions are desperately in need of some form of a large-scale volunteer foundation such as United Credit. United Credit could eventually have an office in each facility to provide for workers, patients and people in need.

A nurse has a personal financial crisis—a doctor has lived beyond his means—a janitor is diagnosed with cancer: all scenarios where United Credit would be there to provide avenues for self help, as well as emergency credit on their United Credit card—credit that is not a loan, not a free hand out, but is reward for real time given to others or time promised to others. There is no reason why anyone has to suffer—the patient or the health care provider.

Since United Credit can never become a welfare system, time promised but not fulfilled would expire the individual's United Credit card until fulfilled (barring forgivable and just circumstances).

The bottom line is this: there is a huge, gaping hole in our system—a canyon that is getting wider and deeper between our providers and the patients. Patients are now treated as commodities or instruments of profit, not only by doctors and providers, but also by medical and drug corporations. Humanitarian values of help and healing have been increasingly stripped from the doctor-patient relationship and the corporate-society relationship—all for the sake of more and more money for those far removed from the actual acts of healing. Until this problem is addressed, nothing will change in our healthcare system. United Credit could potentially recreate the values needed to move towards a truly fair and universal healthcare system.

I propose that a foundation, such as United Credit, root itself from the beginning in the healthcare system. Give every single person the potential to earn healthcare credit if they need it or require it. Most importantly, they should not have to work for a medical institution or hospital to earn this credit—**any**

humanitarian service should suffice. It is equally important to give doctors, nurses and administrators a way to give back to others while earning credit that can benefit them in the ways they may need or desire. Money does not need to change hands. The issue of money is the obvious plague and obstacle to creating a new economic model. This issue can and will be absorbed/transformed by the expanding foundation of United Credit.

Obviously, the insurance and drug corporations would be deathly opposed to any such new economic model for attaining healthcare. However, healthcare for profit is a serious issue that needs to be addressed immediately by Americans. It is our social responsibility to reform and enforce humanitarian morals and values when it comes to taking care of sick, hurt or dying human beings.

United Credit and Education
(Right number 4)

Equal access to educational opportunities; what a concept! Great strides have been made towards more equal access to education but still the capitalistic pangs of profit and greed are bleeding the American educational system to death. For example, no educational facility should be strapped with a mortgage. No city or town should have to struggle to keep an educational facility open. No individual should come out of college with a debt of $100,000 and still be worried about finding a job. Where is the humanity in that? There are many educated and socially concerned people available in our society that could potentially help resolve the education crisis. Just as communities used to get together to build needy families a home, the same communities used to get together to build the school houses. Something was lost in the past 100 years. The quest for material things, comfort and prestige has damaged our souls.

Whether it be intellectual development, vocational development, the humanities or other pursuits, there are people from all these areas who could potentially teach others. This is not to say we could replace teachers in schools and universities. Full time career teachers are irreplaceable. However, we could ease the crisis on so many levels by sharing our knowledge and skills with others if given the opportunity. With the help of United Credit, a skilled trades person could be directed to a vocational school that needs help in teaching the trades: time given by the donor, in exchange for credit received which would be provided by the foundation.

Unemployment is a creation of capitalism. There is no reason why there should be any unemployment. All humans have something to give, but in our current system where job opportunities are continually shrinking, the average person is broken down once unemployed. Self esteem, faith and motivation are often lost after a few short months. The pressure of bills, rising debt and financial worry compounds and the human heart is crushed. This is always the end result of failed capitalism on the personal level.

Where is the compassion, the sharing or the giving? *I say give someone an opportunity to give of themselves at all times and in all circumstances.* Give people the opportunity to educate themselves and improve their lives at all times and in all circumstances. I know people in my home state of Maine that have been unemployed for more than three years. Most of them are on state and local city assistance just to live the most meager of lives in small rooms or boarding homes. Many of them have been on a waiting list for educational help for the duration. However, there are no funds available, as institutions that offer free courses are overwhelmed. Worse of all, there are no organizations that they can turn to for offering their time and energy—time and energy that would allow them to earn educational, health or living expense credit! Now you tell me what is wrong with this system?

Don't get me wrong. I do not think that an organization such as United Credit is the magic cure for society's ills. However, I do see such an organization as a key to creating new economic values and real change in our humanitarianism and social economy.

It is important that an organization such as United Credit take the lead in supporting new areas of education including the development of alternative energy technology, alternative healing and health technology and sustainable living practices. So much of the educational process today is promoting a dying system of ideas and business practices. Our educational system needs to shift drastically and soon. Vocational schools need people to help teach sustainable new home construction—homes that are not dependent on fossil fuels. This kind of knowledge and technology has already been developed and proven but it is not being taught to our children!

Extra credit and support should be extended to educational institutions that offer degrees and certificates in subjects like solar power, hydrogen power, sustainable farming and clean water technology. There are whole new alternative industries on the horizon once progressive educational changes are set in motion.

The days of going into med school for the purpose of six figure incomes have to end. The days of going into law school for money, prestige and power have to end. Education for the individual must be for the benefit of humanity. So many minds, so many talents are never given a chance in America because of the rising costs of education. On the planet, millions and millions of people never even get a glimpse at educational opportunities. I am sure that one day we will realize in the universal community humanity has fallen behind. *Do you really think we are the only race of beings in this vast universe?*

In much of Europe, education like healthcare, is seen as a social responsibility and is provided without debt, loans or financial stress to students. A revolution in American's educational system needs to happen soon. But education starts in the basic values and concepts that children are exposed to from day one. How is the human race going to re-educate its youth away from the capitalistic mindset? That is the most pressing issue of our day. This is the issue that an organization such as United Credit could potentially be so effective in addressing.

Model schools/universities could be created—schools that are set up and run without any money, without any salaries, without any budget deficits. It's not impossible. It is actually quite possible and could be done effectively all over the world. The most important model schools will be the ones that usher in humanitarian education in all the areas mentioned above.

Imagine educational institutions that are set up as intentional communities—self-sustaining with alternative energy, organic farming, universal healthcare and working shops—science labs where exiting new ideas/discoveries could evolve. Students would share in the responsibilities of the educational community—food production, housing, cleaning, etc.—all in exchange for their education and for the creation of a better educational facility/community when they leave. Our concepts about the educational process are going to have to change and evolve as the current world economy continues to spiral out of control. Along with the issues of food and healthcare, education is another important area of the social economy that needs immediate and revolutionary transformation.

UNITED CREDIT AND THE HUMANITIES
(Right number 5)

Hand in hand with education, United Credit would support all aspects of the humanities with special attention to philosophy. In our fast pace technological world, the lack of philosophical education has attributed to the rise in greed, corruption and destruction. Without philosophical education, human beings will struggle to make wise choices, develop spiritually or make meaningful contributions to the sustainability of humanity's existence on this planet. I am not talking about religion. I am talking about ethical and moral principles and values—universal truths—humanitarian concerns. Our educational institutions have, in many cases, thrown out philosophical education altogether. In more recent decades, we are producing technologically educated people that have no ethical, moral or spiritual foundation to apply their knowledge. Do you realize what the implications of this are? At this rate, humanity could turn into intellectual robots reproducing in laboratories, taking pill form supplements as meals and mining other planets for metals to supply its technological needs. Believe me, this is not a ridiculous assertion—not at all. These types of races likely already exist out there as other worlds that may have already gone down the road we are currently on.

The key to changing our fate lies in the humanities—the arts, music, philosophy, literature, etc. It is the human soul—the human heart that we are here to advance—not just the human mind. Remember my friend Robert—the Veteran artist? Had there been some organization like United Credit that could have recognized his real talent and his "humanity", things may have turned out very different for him. Because of the lack of the humanities in education, many people in the world today are wandering aimlessly through life with no inspiration and no purpose. Millions of Americans go to work every day and struggle not to lose their souls in business/corporate situations where principles of profit and gain eclipse out any philosophic, moral or ethical concepts of human economy.

If a child is neglected and given television and violent video games, what could we expect from the potential outcome other than depression, unhappiness and, in some cases, violent behavior? However, if a child is given attention, art and music, do you suppose the potential outcome could be happiness, creativity and non-violence? There has been such a disconnection between public education, private education and family life over the past 30 years. Parents send their children to school and barely get involved in what they are learning. When the child comes home, the TV, video games, social media and the internet take-over. Where are the opportunities for children to experience the humanities in our society?

Is this part of the great corporate take-over? Are we going to lose whole generations of children to the technological beast? With the explosion of cell phones, mobile internet, personal electronic games and social media, society is going virtual—virtual meaning: NOT REAL! Eventually, the virtual, unreal world would lead to a soulless society.

What happens when people lose their soul? You don't have to look around very far to find an answer. America has well over 2 million people incarcerated currently, many of them guilty of crimes directly related to the loss of meaning and soul purpose somewhere along the line. The perfect example is a young urban teenager with no place to turn but to gangs, drugs and violence. Isn't that what we have really been fostering in this country? Have you noticed the violent video games and movies that are the best sellers to our youth? We are creating a terrible reality in the name of profit and greed. Where are the humanities with our youth? It's no wonder that our young people are acting out violence and shootings in their schools and among their peers.

All across this planet, people are losing their humanity. It is imperative that new social programs are instituted that promote the arts and humanities. United Credit would solicit artists, writers, musicians, philosophers, teachers, potters—craftspeople of all types, and creative thinkers to give time and energy to helping children develop with the humanities.

Education in the humanities leads to humanitarian behavior.

Humanity evolves meaningfully only through pure creative impulse. Creativity has been increasingly suppressed in many societies, while in other societies, creativity cannot even take hold due to the basic issues of starvation, war and political repression. Whenever possible, United Credit would support all aspects of the humanities, especially in terms of youth programming and education. Food for the body must be accompanied by or followed with food for the soul.

UNITED CREDIT AND FREE ENERGY
(Right number 6)

All people have a right to share the energy resources and energy technologies available to modern civilization. When Nicola Tesla brought AC electrical current to Thomas Edison's laboratory at the turn of the last century, his vision was not Edison Light and Power. His vision was for free energy and for the advancement of humanity into a new age. He was against selling power. Tesla actually developed more advanced energy harnessing and transmission methods that could have led to a planet wide, free energy system! It was business tycoons like J. P. Morgan that saw the opportunity for great wealth through the control of energy resources. One hundred years later, we still have utility poles cluttering the landscape holding up electric wires that sell power to homes and businesses. Man, did humanity get stuck on this one.

Nicola Tesla also realized the opportunities for free energy that would come through the development of his discoveries with electric motors, electric charging systems and advanced energy harnessing. But Tesla saw the opportunities and advancements of energy technologies as a basic right to all people. He was a humanitarian who envisioned a society based on free energy and, because of that, he was repressed and eventually confined to a hotel room where he died without ever seeing his humanitarian visions realized. Powerful people who were solidifying their corporate control of energy resources were afraid of Tesla and saw to it that his humanitarian visions (and discoveries) of universally free energy systems were never realized.

The control and manipulation of energy technology and energy resources has had a repressive and dark hold on human advancement. The continued dependence on coal, oil and natural gas is having disastrous environmental consequences. Putting aside the carbonization of our atmosphere and the drastic reductions in photosynthesis, the shear mass reductions in the planet's crustal plates is monumental and is already causing gravitational imbalances. These imbalances have already become evident in recent years with massive crustal plate movements, such as the recent crustal slide off the coast of Japan becoming more frequent. From both an environmental and economic point of view, the dependence on coal, oil and natural gas is suicidal.

The world's industrial/military base is so linked to fossil fuels that it would likely take a whole generation before a complete shift to renewable/free energy systems could happen —and that's if we started shifting now! I don't think we have 40 years. There are leading scientists that are predicting total environmental collapse in 30 or 40 years if we continue down this road of fossil fuel dependence. It is extremely important that a new economic model address all aspects of renewable/free energy technology as soon as possible.

United Credit would need to support research into alternative and renewable energy sources as a top priority. Extensive credit and resources would need to be set aside for companies making discoveries and advancements in solar power, hydrogen power, geothermal, wind, electromagnetic and other areas of alternative energy research. In 2011, the technology for self-charging cell phones became a reality. Self-charging energy systems that can pull power out of the atmosphere from radio waves, electromagnetics and sound waves are no longer science fiction. If research into such discoveries is fully funded and heavily promoted, every appliance we use, including our transportation vehicles, may be able to run endlessly without any fuel or any recharging! This is Tesla technology that has finally broken the ice with cell phones. The question is: will it be suppressed?

Self-charging cars are on the way. The advancements in piezoelectrics as well as many other areas of capturing and storing energy are on the brink of changing our world forever. These are the areas of energy research that need to be funded and accelerated! Had these areas been funded and supported decades ago, humanity would now be leaving fossil fuels in the ground where they belong.

I realize that radical shifts in energy technology are needed in the larger, corporate arena but there are many practical ways United Credit could jump start the shift away from fossil fuels. One of the most important ground level projects could be creating homes that are off the grid—homes that have energy systems linked to solar, geothermal and other eco-friendly sustainable technologies. Creating homes that use absolutely no carbon-based fuel could become an amazing industry. Imagine the healthy and sustainable economic activity that would be created by such projects.

Funding and credit extended to all levels of solar research would be extremely important. From small solar conversions to large ones, every light bulb that is un-plugged from electricity would be measurable progress!

Funding and credit could be extended to alternative transportation methods and research. Transportation is another industry on the verge of an economic boom, once we really start making the full shift away from fossil fuels.

Funding and credit could be extended to *Zero Energy* home construction as mentioned earlier. There is no need to pump oil and gas in order to sustain home or business climates—not with the knowledge and technology that is now available. Advancements in *Zero Energy* home construction may end up creating an amazing new era of economic prosperity.

Imagine for a moment that United Credit acquires a foreclosed farm and sets up an educational institution on the farm teaching people how to live free of fossil fuels, grow organic food and come together creating sustainable living. Imagine farms like this all over the country. I can see places like this being incredibly valuable in dealing with so many social issues such as hunger, homelessness, unemployment, community welfare, etc. One might think that in today's corporate world this is a fancy dream. However, in the future, we will be back to square one creating these kinds of farms. The drive by big corporations to control the food production will end disastrously and leave humanity struggling to recreate. *I am sure that, in the interim, the ideas presented in this book will not be welcomed by certain corporate entities.*

Nevertheless, the world needs an organization like United Credit not only to come forth with a new economic philosophy and a new economic value system, but one that requires a powerful humanitarian vision for a truly fair and sustainable future economy.

UNITED CREDIT AND ENVIRONMENTAL PROTECTION
(Right number 7)

One of the most important social/economic issues of all that needs to be addressed by any new economic model is that of our environment. I think it is becoming increasingly evident that all of the world's resources are limited and that the overuse of them is causing great harm to the planet's ecosystem. The most self-evident example of this is the petroleum industry and the dependence of the world economy on oil, coal and gas. Considering the seriousness of this issue, I think it is worthy of a few paragraphs:

Coal and oil are the remains of past life—compressed plant, animal and perhaps ancient human remains. Sudden catastrophes tend to bury large amounts of these remains in low places in the form of sludge and peat. As this material is buried over time, it is heated and compressed into coal and then into oil. It takes about 100 feet of compressed vegetation and animal mass to make one level foot of peat. It takes about 100 feet of compressed peat to make one level foot of coal or oil. Oil reserves have been found that are hundreds of feet deep. That is a lot of compressed, once living matter! Modern society now feeds off these remains of past life and is literally "raising the dead" into the atmosphere by the burning of fossil fuels.

What is almost insanely ironic about this is that we are feeding off of past planetary catastrophes to create a new one —a potential catastrophe beyond our wildest imagination. What does this mean for humanity in the coming years? The Earth is currently balanced very precariously at a 23.5-degree tilt on its rotational axis as it revolves around the Sun within the great gravitational belt that extends outward into the solar system. With the combination of the moon, planets and all the other gravitational effects, the Earth has maintained its delicate axis balance for thousands of years—ever since the last major gravitational shakeup which resulted in global floods, volcanic upheaval and the sliding of continental plates.

It is the mass of the Earth in the proportions given by nature in relation to all the solar system's gravitational fields that determines the balance and stability of the axis tilt and the north-south pole alignment. If we change any of the major mass ratios of the earth, including the mass ratios of our planet's crustal mass, it only stands to reason that a major shift in planetary balance will follow. Even a minor shift in the Earth's polar axis would be cataclysmic and disastrous for human existence as we know it.

The removal rates of coal and oil from the crustal mass of the northern hemisphere is reaching epidemic proportions. Aside from the fact that we are completely destroying nature's perfectly tuned "carbon sink" which allowed for our oxygen rich atmosphere and the development of mammals and humans on this planet, we are rapidly turning the tables of planetary stability. The northern hemisphere is no longer balanced with the southern hemisphere. Humanity is pumping oil and removing coal from the northern hemisphere at an ever-increasing pace. The planet's axis is becoming more unstable. We are not looking at centuries or decades before a major crustal shift unfolds on this planet. We are looking at years, and perhaps just a few years. It is imperative that we stop the removal of the Earth's crustal mass as soon as possible, or we are going to be witnessing more and more earthquakes and tsunamis like those in recent years—not to mention the destruction of our atmosphere.

Besides the environmental destruction being brought on

by the petroleum industry, there are even greater environmental issues in the areas of clean water, ocean dumping, farming practices, genetically altered seeds, pesticides, etc. One can safely say that all of these economic practices are driven by the quest for money—by greed. All of these economic practices are void of any guiding moral, spiritual or humanitarian principles. This is what has to change. Humanity cannot continue to create social economies that do not have a sound philosophical/ethical foundation. Without moral/ethical foundations, social economies are easily held in bondage by democratic capitalist models that dominate much of the developed world—capitalist models that dance around or completely ignore environmental issues.

Any shift towards new economic models must take into consideration environmental protection. Economies must be built within the limits of sustainable resources and environmental practices. This can be accomplished most effectively by starting at the grass roots/community level. One can only imagine the possible opportunities that could be instantly created by shifting away from an economy that hinges its growth and success on destructive environmental practices. I can foresee an organization, such as United Credit, working with communities on many levels to foster environmentally-friendly economic activities. United Credit would initiate business and economic activity that protects our water, forests, and air, as well as the future ability to exist on this planet.

Examples of environmental friendly economics:

Solar/electric – There is absolute and confirmed technology in this area. Solar collection stations could be installed in neighborhoods to supply homes, business and all local (electric) transportation needs.

Solar/compost – Solar heating systems could be linked to organic gardens and greenhouses—not only providing hot water and heat to community buildings, but to homes as well.

Focused Recycling – There is so much more that all communities could be doing in this area and actually, there are many more possible economic opportunities that could be generated by conscious, careful recycling: managing compost for organic farming, turning waste plastics back into usable products, funding of sustainable community projects through recycling profits, etc.

Green Building and Construction – Not nearly enough planning or consideration for sustainable resources and/or use of toxic products is happening in the construction industry. There are hundreds of new economic opportunities in this field.

Water Filtration – Not only could there be new opportunities providing clean and safe water to families—there are opportunities in the area of providing cleaner rivers and lakes: designing and building natural filtration systems in nature, etc.

Organic Farming – As mentioned already, this is obviously a huge issue—people need healthy food. Economic opportunities in the areas of seed preservation, GMO free food, orchard management, bee farming, etc. are extremely important. While there is currently great corporate resistance to this, we cannot ignore the potential deadly consequences of not investing nor supporting organic farming.

Forest Preservation – There is such a political/government resistance to certain potential revolutions in farming. Farming of crops (hemp), for example, could completely provide all the resources for a major portion of the nation's paper, cloth and building product needs without ever having to cut down another tree. It is no secret that in many areas of this country, as well as the world, forest management is poor to negligible.

With all of the above-mentioned examples, there are countless opportunities to create new economic activity. But it all has to start with new economic philosophies that are grounded in humanitarian principles: something that is completely void in capitalism. In all areas of food production, energy, transportation, construction and economic commerce, America is failing. It is our social responsibility to not only take care of each other, but to take care of our environment. If we are aware of an economic activity that is destroying the renewability of a resource, destroying a third world community or an environment, then it is our moral responsibility to stop supporting it. This being said, humanity is in for some big changes in coming decades.

Part 3

United Credit and Social Responsibility

Social/Economic Responsibility

There are many levels of failed social responsibility that United Credit will have to address as the foundation grows and expands—individual, community, political, business and corporate. The individual and community aspects of social responsibility will be addressed every time United Credit issues credit to individuals, or directs resources to places in need, thereby creating a new economic model that provides real and immediate opportunities for those in need rather than handing out free assistance. Addressing the issues of social responsibility in today's capitalist/corporate economy will be one of the most difficult challenges of United Credit. This is a challenge for any new economic model. However, if adopted, an economic "Bill of Rights" could become a powerful set of codes for creating social responsibility on all levels.

The practice of amassing wealth—on any level, personal or corporate—would need to come under strong moral and ethical scrutiny. Human economic activity cannot continue indefinitely without sustainability or without long-term visions. Human economy cannot survive without ultimately becoming responsible for the health of its whole body—its whole people. Today, we have many corporations (often joined with political forces) that are running rampant on this planet. They are not only destroying land, air and water resources; they are destroying societies without any concern for humans or the long-term implications of their economic practices.

Most all American corporations have failed in the area of social responsibility. Hundreds of examples could be given but I will only cite a couple: over the past 30 or 40 years, there has been a mass corporate exodus out of this country in most all areas of manufacturing to developing countries due to cheap foreign labor, non existing regulations of toxic chemicals, no safety regulations and no social mandates for employee healthcare. Does anybody realize the moral and ethical implications being created by this kind of business? How many American consumers are aware of the fact that 28 woman and children, already working in deplorable conditions making around 15 cents an hour, were burned to death in a fire that raged through an un-regulated Bangladesh sweat shop late in 2010 while making brand named clothes commonly sold in American chain stores? Perhaps this aspect of textile manufacturing should have never left this country in the first place. If true economic success had been about the town or community that once was home to that textile mill rather than about maximized profits for a few, things might have been different.

What has happened with many American corporations over the past few decades is that they have in fact abandoned the communities and families, which gave them their start, their name and their wealth. In many cases, some of these corporations were poisoning the local environments causing serious health effects, resulting in increased employee healthcare costs. Rather than commit to helping the communities (which had sustained them in the first place) with their healing, development and growth, many corporations decided to pack up and leave. Economically, this was a grave mistake for America and for the world.

Morally and ethically, it would have been better for American industry to stay put and deal with the challenging issues of corporate/capitalist growth and expansion. First and foremost, it would have led to greater profit sharing. Secondly, the environmental protection issues would have had to be addressed more aggressively leading to advancements in clean industry technologies rather than the toxic dumping we see happening in the third world countries today. Thirdly, corporations would have seen the need to support communities around them—the families of their employees—in order to create better and healthier societies. Finally, the issue of social/economic responsibility could have been addressed head on rather than ignored for the sake of mass profits for a few individuals.

It's bad enough that a corporation fails in its national/cultural social responsibilities but when a corporation goes into another country and irreversibly damages their land, their resource base and their social economy—it becomes more than serious—it becomes a crime against humanity. This is where we are at today; failed social responsibility on a global level and massive corporate criminal behavior.

Publicly traded, limited liability corporations have no reason to be socially responsible. This type of institution is the perfect manifestation of capitalism, as there are virtually no checks and balances to corporate activities. Shareholders are far removed from the corporate acts. Directors are protected by massive legal defenses. Corporations are thus free to exploit workers, poison and destroy environments and manipulate national/international community economies. If an individual should ever commit such criminal acts, they would be sent to prison. This scenario is only getting worse by the month as corporations exercise greater and greater influence in the government sectors of world societies.

This is especially true within the military/industrial corporations. The truth is most of the business/sales practices of the military/industrial corporations are completely devoid of any moral or ethical considerations. It is a sad state of affairs to support the potentially negative economic activity that could bring all of humanity to its knees, simply by arming every rogue militia, military and every political cause to the hilt. More money is spent and more economic activity is generated on military related business, wars, nuclear missiles, and the like, than on any other economic activity on the planet.

It all seems like a problem too huge to tackle, but United Credit could implement many programs and incentives that might help businesses and corporations change their social economic behavior. First and foremost, a scale of moral and ethical economic behavior has to be developed over time. United Credit would advocate for a system like this and companies would all need to be rated according to their responsibility to society, community productivity, environmental protection and their commitment to humanitarian advancement. This one act of economic reformation could potentially become the most powerful of all acts of economic reformation. Accountability and transparency in all areas of social wealth management is absolutely critical.

United Credit could potentially reward companies that adopt or support farms and local gardens, as well as those that give discounts to people in need of food and medicines. Companies that commit to going green, offering world hunger/housing relief or other humanitarian services could be rewarded with credit and human resources. Once a corporation makes a commitment to green practices, for example, whole areas of economic growth are opened up—new jobs are created. The shift toward social responsibility has already started in

American society with a few wealthy individuals realizing the importance of transferring their wealth to humanitarian causes. It is not enough however as more change needs to happen throughout the entire corporate/business world. An organization such as United Credit could foster the needed steady and gradual change by simply working with and supporting companies that are willing to evolve away from the old economic model.

Is it meaningful social responsibility when a company installs a gym or health food bar in its work zone, while that same company is paying top CEO's millions while, at the same time, is poisoning third world environments? What about the investment/banking companies that are backhandedly siphoning off the personal wealth of this economy in the first place? Look at what the lack of a social accountability in corporate business has done to our National economy and the world economy. Ultimately, the final rewards for the social economy will come when companies restructure their profit disbursements, adopt moral and ethical social/environmental policies and realize that economic activity is not meant to benefit just a few but *all* of society.

By now, there may be a few who would really call me a socialist. However, I would refute that one hundred percent. My vision is of a golden age of peace and prosperity. Do you think we can get there from our current economic systems? One of the definitions of socialism is "the social ownership of the means of production, as well as property". Most all socialist societies have ended up with centralized ownership and management of the means of production and the produced assets by non-local governmental bureaucracies. I am not advocating traditional socialism. As a later chapter will reveal, United Credit would be set up under a charter that advocates non-ownership of the above mentioned. United Credit would be developed as a collective management organization—a humanitarian-based economic model that rejects ownership principles and fosters responsible stewardship of all property/resources, always transferring "ownership" to future generations.

One of the most important social economic issues of today is the lack of vision—the lack of real purpose and meaning regarding the future. What is the collective goal of everything we are creating? What kind of society are we going to leave for our children and our grandchildren? What we have in today's economy is a free-for-all with not much regard for future generations. This the primary moral/ethical core issue facing all world societies and each of us as individuals. **Social responsibility begins with a vision of what our economic activity is meant to create.**

We no longer live in isolated communities ruled by lords and barons. How we as individuals act and how businesses and corporations act impacts the whole planet and determines the balance of economic prosperity for everyone. We live in a different world these days—a world where it's becoming more obvious that resources are limited, where everything that happens is instantly known to all, where suffering is more evident and where what we are creating will be right in front of us all the time. One of the challenges facing United Credit from the beginning will be promoting a future vision towards which all economic activity must be aimed. In formulating a social responsibility scale by which businesses and corporations would be rated, the future goals and ultimate social benefit must be considered.

On the individual level, social responsibility has not had a great track record either and that is largely due to education and social conditioning. This is the area where that an organization such as United Credit could have its first impact. The most fundamental principle of United Credit is the economic value based on human actions and deeds, helping and sharing with others rather than acquiring for personal gain. This is the seed philosophy. A transformation in thought and ideas about material value and ownership will happen once people realize that there are other ways to create economic prosperity—*prosperity without money.*

Individual social/economic responsibility means that each person must understand the implications of their social/economic behaviors including what and how much we consume—where it comes from and the social/economic imprint that it creates. The myth of the American Dream (where everybody can have what they want—all the money and wealth that they can create) has to end eventually. Imagine 6 billion people on the planet all trying to live the *American Dream*! We would have a huge problem. We already have a huge problem. As the populations in countries such as China and India try to create their own individual wealth and prosperity to mirror Americans, the planet's resources are unable to sustain these lifestyles and resulting economies.

The model of individual gain and prosperity without regard for society or a humanitarian vision is a dying horse and humanity is currently beating it to death. The model that is needed is one that has a moral and ethical foundation for shared social/ economic prosperity. As the world economic crises continues to unfold, each one of us is going to have to take a more critical look at our everyday economic activity—what we buy, who and what we support when we consume, what we give back to the whole, and most importantly, what future vision we are promoting. Because of the many decades of unchecked wealth and materialism in developed Nations,

America and Europe now have a moral responsibility to the rest of the world—a responsibility to create new economic models that take into account a truly humanitarian purpose and vision for the future of world societies. I believe that America, at this moment, is now ready for this great challenge. Many of the world economies are looking to our country to set the pace and the foundations to real economic change. God help us if we fail at this responsibility.

Grace Credits

Unfortunately, we are living in a sick and dying world, becoming increasingly ruled by chemical/pharmaceutical corporations that are not supporting the creation of a healthy society. There are many difficult social issues to deal with regarding sickness, terminal diseases and mental illness. There are several social issues regarding the handicapped and the disabled, as well as issues regarding the elderly and retirement system that need to addressed. There will always be a percentage of people who will not be able to make meaningful contributions to society. They will need temporary, and in many cases, permanent help—*grace credits*. We all have a social responsibility to help those in need. In addition, we all have the responsibility to help those who have worked hard and given to others all their lives.

I submit as well that there is a large amount of welfare/economic assistance being granted in our society to people who are not sick or disabled—those who could give their time and effort on many levels to help others. This type of assistance could account for 30 or 40% of all public welfare programs. Not having a method or program established to match people in need with ways they could give back to society is a real problem. Currently, our society pays out welfare to people who would be able to work if given the opportunity and then pays out again to care for people who truly need *grace credits*. In other words, there is a balancing of economy when a different value system is applied to a welfare system and you begin matching people in need with people who are well and able. People do not really want something for nothing. People do want to feel worthy. Give them opportunities to help others while earning needed credit when they have fallen on hard times!

I suppose this opens up a whole debate about how and to whom grace credits should be extended—how it will be supported and who will manage and make decisions about grace credits to fund those in need. Right from the beginning, part of the mission of United Credit will be to match people willing to serve and give of their time with those people in need. Early on, credit extended will have to be drawn from a collective fund established at the start.

There could be many creative solutions to the issue of *grace credits*. One idea that comes to mind is that all people coming into the system—donors and participants—would contribute to the grace credit fund. People earning credit from the organization could choose whether or not they wanted 2 or 3% of their earned credit to go to the grace credit account. On the other end, potential wealthy donors (companies or individuals) coming into the system could be given donor options, which would disperse *grace credit* donations fairly within the foundation. Some of these people may not need all the credit they earn, or may not need credit from the organization at all. Potentially a bank of grace credits could be quickly developed, which combined with the real bank of human resources, could go a long way towards helping those really in need.

To be clear, accumulated grace credits may be understood by some as another form of money. However, if this argument is made, then the value of United *credits* would be traced to something real and meaningful—actions/deeds completed or given and/or shared material resources. This would be a radical departure from the monetary value system we are using now, by which money is being printed from "thin air". This is the most important point of this writing: An accumulation or bank of United *credits* would ultimately have a history of creating something good and needed for society. It would be a *measurable type of humanitarian wealth* that could be a great transforming force for social economies.

Across the board in all areas of United Credit funding and programs, the grace credit bank could grow and flourish, creating new kinds of programs for housing, food, renewable energy and healthcare. Imagine a new assisted living facility built by donated land, labor and materials—sustained with non-fossil fuel and self-renewing energy systems—managed by a force of United Credit time donors such as doctors, nurses, aids and maintenance people. This is the economy of the future. Whether we like it or not, humans that survive the coming world economic and political warfare will have to work together to help each other, not only to recreate their communities, but to create meaningful and spiritually rich societies. Humanity has come too far to collapse into a planet of money-grubbing apes!

Creating a social welfare system that is rooted in humanitarian values and humanitarian action is really what *grace credits* is all about. Every person coming into the United Credit foundation, in one way or another, would be contributing to the collective bank of grace credit. This collective bank of grace credit would not be a bank of money, mutual funds, stocks or bonds. It will not exist in any form that can be traded, borrowed against or de-valued. The collective bank of grace credit would represent both earned and deserved humanitarian assistance in times of need. As a form of humanitarian currency, any credit given or extended by United Credit including grace credits would exist only through the giving of others—thus helping to establish economic prosperity based on real and meaningful human value.

One of the important issues to be addressed while developing the idea of *grace credits* is that of elderly retirement. Currently, healthy and comfortable retirement is very much linked to money and wealth. There are many retirement communities around this country and the world that are wonderful to live in if a person can ultimately afford them. United Credit would focus on creating retirement communities that are not only linked to sustainable living, but that are supported and funded by the collective bank of human and material resources. It is not fair that a hard working trade/service person, laborer or anyone else should end up cold and homeless at the end of their life only because they could never afford to build any retirement funds. If societies work to build safe, guaranteed and fully supported communities for their elderly, then they are actually working to build healthier societies across the board for the whole of their populations.

Communities for the elderly could be fully linked to the new social economy. *Retirement* could be redefined by activities that not only allow for rest and enjoyment but activities that require a level of support, guidance and help for the younger generations in whatever capacities people are able to fulfill. Most people do not want to be forced out of community involvement simply because they lose their jobs or they are too old to keep up in the ever changing work place. The experience and knowledge of the elderly can and should be harvested by all communities in ways that provide dignity and purpose. There is a vast realm of opportunities is this area that are ripe to be developed.

Every single person on the planet has a vested interest in supporting a collective fund of grace credits. We all have parents that will enter their elderly years, and eventually we ourselves will enter our own elderly years. We all know someone that is sick, dying, handicapped, or disabled. It is only natural to support a foundation that promises to provide for those in need without creating economic burdens. There are many creative ways to fund, enrich and sustain such a foundation. The current systems that are based on taxes (money) are bound to fail as the value of money continues to evaporate into the thin air—the thin air that it was in the first place! Humanity needs a bank of credit (units of value) that are real—*real* people ready to help, *real* food stocks, *real* housing stocks, *real* medical stocks—a rich reserve of *real* resources. Creating and sustaining such a reserve is the one of the mission statements of United Credit.

Once such a reserve of human and material wealth is established, it only needs fostering and care by all future generations. There would be no loss in value, no risky investment and no political control. We are talking about *real* things: homes, food, human skills, human giving and sharing—a whole new set of economic values—aspects of existence that are at the core of our survival and happiness as humans. How do we create this new economy? How do we get there from here?

TOUGH LOVE

This is a tough one! How would an organization like United Credit handle people who absolutely are not willing to help others or give anything? What about the drug addict that does not want to change and does not want to rehabilitate? What about the prison population and criminals? What about the millionaire banker who clings to his wealth, property and greed? Humanitarian transformation in any of the above scenarios will not be easy or magically addressed. However, there are a lot of small steps—programs and ideas—that United Credit could support from the start, which could plants some seeds of social/economic transformation.

Before confronting any of the above social dilemmas, United Credit would need a solid organization and a proven track record of helping individuals, organizations and businesses. Dealing with substance abuse is, in the best of circumstances, a tough social challenge. Often, people recovering from substance abuse struggle for years to rebuild their lives. The best healers in our society are people who have healed themselves. United Credit could focus on programs and opportunities that allow recovered people to work directly with those in recovery. Obviously, there are such programs out there like Alcoholics Anonymous that serve a great need. However, these programs can be given a new type of support—allowing people who are serving to help others earn United credit—a much needed resource base (car, home, education, etc.) for those who are rebuilding their lives.

One of the biggest failures of our social rehabilitation system is the lack of opportunities to earn needed material resources, which often results in relapse, and in the case of convicted people, more crime on the streets. If people are provided opportunities that allow them to help improve the lives of others, while at the same time improving their own lives, a greater measure of self-worth and success will be the result. Then of course there are countless opportunities for doctors, nurses, health institutions, counselors, etc. to come into the system, thus building their bank of United credit while shifting towards more humanitarian service.

It would not take more than a year or two for United Credit to build a bank of human and material resources that are both appealing and desirable to almost any person. We are not talking about ***money-based*** *credit, we are talking about something far more valuable in the long run—something that would never be affected by inflation, bank failures, or economic collapse. We are not talking about something owned by the top wealthiest 450 individuals in the world and then loaned back to us by organizations like the Federal Reserve. We are talking about providing people with a blanket security system that provides for the needs of all people who are willing to enter the humanitarian age of helping others. What good is money if it does not allow you to take care of your basic needs? What good is money if it ends up trapping you into a lifetime of debt and worry? What good is money if it is never enough to allow you to develop and flourish culturally and spiritually? What United Credit would potentially create is a measure of wealth in a different way—a way that transforms the false economy serving the rich into a real economy serving the people.*

No doubt, for the next few generations, there will be people who are not willing to help others and/or are not able to be helped—those who are committed to their addictions. There will have to be a measure of tough love in any new social/economic system that develops in the coming years. United Credit will have to walk away from these individuals. There will be committed criminals whom are not willing to change or serve humanity in any meaningful way. Institutions that house these types of people will need to continue to provide the means to human transformation and healing; and this can be done with new ideas and programs that may inspire the deep-rooted desires that most all humans have to help others. I truly believe that every single human being has a need to give. Our society has not fostered this aspect of humanness in recent generations.

More educational programs are needed in the prison system that link directly with a real job which has value in the social/ economic culture on the outside, even if the prisoner is still on the inside. What about medical transcriptions for example? What about graphics, art, music? Do you think we can ever find an end to the dilemma of expanding overcrowded prisons in our country if we don't find new approaches to rehabilitation? United Credit would solicit educators to give time and energy to penal institutions. United Credit would help find the resources needed to support new programs. Once again, United Credit would have to walk away from those individuals who consciously turn their backs on humanitarian transformation. But even in that walking away, United Credit would support programs that put these individuals to use filling larger social needs.

Offering work/educational programs to incarcerated persons should be coupled with opportunities to earn United credit while they are still wards of the state/federal prison system. This would allow them to build and plan for a real chance to start a new life once they are released, as well as help them to gain greater self-esteem and self-respect. If given the opportunity to help others while still incarcerated, I believe that many convicted offenders would have a greater chance to change and rehabilitate. A portion of inmate earned credit could be designated to the collective *grace credit* fund, which allows for some repayment to society and a meaningful form of retribution.

A huge part of any *tough love* stand taken by an organization such as United Credit will involve recognizing individuals who are not interested in helping others on any level. After repeated attempts to offer assistance, education or opportunities for change, United Credit would have to move forward without them. People are going to fall through the cracks and its going to take a few generations to transform our often self-serving and wealth-serving economy into a human based and future orientated economy.

America's social welfare, in its current manifestation is not serving the greater social good. All economic resources shared by our social assistance programs with those in need (those who are well and able) should be earned—thus creating huge restoration in the areas of human dignity and pride. All social welfare programs should be rich with opportunities to give back and help others, even in the most simple and basic examples. There are a multitude of welcoming opportunities waiting for human resources in our society.

Once again, the mission of United Credit would be to remove paper (valueless) money from our economy and replace it with a form of economic compensation that is rich with human purpose, social improvement and humanitarian advancement.

Freedom and Social/Economic Justice

One of the most important social issues sweeping global societies today is the need for freedom. Whether it be freedom from corrupt dictators, freedom from poverty and oppression or freedom from over-riding debt and worry, people are rising up in increasing numbers and in increasing countries. *Freedom* is a wonderful a thing and an aspect of being that all humans deserve; but freedom comes with a price. That price is social responsibility.

Without a doubt, the model of freedom that world societies are looking to is the American model of freedom. While this model has its amazing aspects and opportunities, it also has great perils and pitfalls. It's a model of freedom that is still in its infancy—undeveloped and unrealized in terms of equality in social economies. It's a model that is held within the bounds of capitalism and so called *free* enterprise. American society has not yet evolved into a society of real freedom. Millions of Americans are losing their jobs, their homes—all their material aspects of *freedom*. The interesting aspect of this is that most of these people never felt they had much freedom in the first place while they lived under mountains of debt, unhappiness and financial worry.

The freedoms that all Americans have enjoyed are freedom of thought and religion. The freedoms that some Americans have enjoyed are that of travel, career, healthcare and opportunities for wealth. The freedoms that only a few Americans have enjoyed are life styles free of financial worry. The freedom that no American has enjoyed is the freedom of a life not dictated by **money**. Without money, American freedom is limited to freedom of thought and religion. Unfortunately, freedom of thought and religion does not feed, clothe or provide shelter for the body.

I can understand that for most people, it may be hard to envision freedom in a society that does not use money as units of economic value—concepts that we are accustomed to. However, it is possible to create a *free* society that prints no money, exchanges no money or amasses no money. It is possible to create a society that manages the collective resources in a fair and equitable way, allowing each person the same freedoms enjoyed by all the others. A concept such as this represents a more evolved nature of freedom. I can never be free while my brother or sister is bound in chains of financial desperation. The wealthy corporate executive can never be free while young woman and children (such as third world employees) are slaving 12 hours a day in horrendous factory conditions making two or perhaps three dollars a day, while trapped in endless capitalist induced poverty and social degradation. In such cases, the rich corporate executive has actually enslaved his own soul to some eventual karmic retribution.

Here is the most important point about freedom: Where does my right for individual freedom—to do what I want, amass the wealth I want and have, eat and travel as I want—infringe upon the freedoms of others or upon society as a whole? Freedom must be balanced with social justice. This is the biggest revolutionary issue of this decade as humanity is now witnessing around the planet. The explosion in social media has allowed people to taste the freedoms and life styles of those in other countries (especially the more developed countries), and naturally they want those freedoms and life styles. Whole populations are standing up to wealthy dictators. They are demanding more shared freedoms in every sense—economic, intellectual, religious and political.

Whether the current world leaders like it or not, the old system of money and wealth acquisition is dying. Our corporate civilization is like a giant pyramid with the rich sitting at the apex and the struggling/poor masses making up the base. If the masses cannot get enough to eat or can no longer bear the pressure pushing down from the top, the whole structure will collapse. Humanity is either going to move into a new age of economic prosperity for all, or we are going to be held back in a terrible dark age by the murderous barons of selfish greed. It is an exciting but dangerous time we live in. The new philosophy and poten-tial solutions that a foundation such as United Credit could bring to our transforming world economy may be of immense value. They may help to create a bridge, or at least part of the bridge, to get to an era of real world peace and prosperity.

I do not see my book or the concepts put forth with United Credit as the miraculous solution to the world's economic woes. I do see it as a potential bridge and I welcome any and all philosophical/economic ideas and improvements by others to the concepts presented here.

Freedom verses social justice:

An organization such as United Credit that is founded on humanitarian economics could actually help create a model of social and individual freedom not yet experienced by humanity. First and foremost, the very act of helping others can be a profound, soul-freeing experience. More importantly, working within a higher vision towards the welfare of the collective whole is even more freeing—freedom that is *real* and *meaningful* has nothing to do with money and wealth!

Social justice can never be achieved as long as people continue to strive for wealth. Social justice is, at its core, an economic issue. It has always been an economic issue. If you study history, you will find that most of the past wars, revolutions and human conflicts began with issues related to the control of or the distribution of resources (food, water, medicines, etc.) in societies. True social justice begins with the simple act of sharing and helping others. A lasting social economy begins with the same acts of sharing and helping others. The aspects of human nature that oppose social justice (greed, selfishness, etc.) need to be rooted out of any future attempts to create a lasting social economy.

United Credit would understand and promote this philosophy from the beginning, but would also work to build in safeguards to discourage negative human behavior: greed and selfishness. Because of these negative human traits, there have been very few examples of successful and sustainable social economies in past history. In recent history, there have been a few that started with the vision of a fair social economy, but ended up being ruled by greedy, wealthy dictators, or corrupt politicians. That is also the case today. We have seen countless social revolutions in the past couple of generations, but almost every single one of them ended the same way—economic imbalance and political corruption. America is a young country that also started with a vision of social justice and a fair social economy. However, in only two hundred years, we have fallen victim to some of the worse examples of greed and selfishness that have ever existed on the planet. American corporate greed is raping the earth, destroying other cultures and choking its own citizens with debt, poisons, lies, and thievery. *How did this happen?* How did America collapse into a social economy that has its social justice defined by capitalism?

Social justice, as stated earlier, comes down to economics. All people rightfully need their basic economic rights fulfilled. People have the right to food, shelter, healthcare, education, etc. A society that is not providing these basic rights will fail. America is on a path of terrible social destruction, especially if nothing is done to change the present course of our social economy. In the first place, you cannot have a government bailing out wealthy banks and corporations that have violated the trust of Americans. The seeds of revolution are being planted with these types of economic policies. The seeds of revolution are being planted by our own political parties who are deadlocked in partisan battles controlled by corporate special interest. *Where is the fairness? Where is the vision for a better social economy? Where is the social justice?*

We must create an organization such as United Credit and fund it fully! We can call it by any name, but I call it United Credit because I realize that the word *credit* **bridges** the present and future economy. Our definition of credit should shift away from "debt" and should be replaced with "deserve" and "reserved". The important thing is to begin creating a new social economy as soon as possible. As I write these words, there are countries falling into revolution that are going to need a new economic models, new economic philosophies and organizations that can provide for them. The young people of the world are reaching out for freedom and economic justice. Somehow, the leaders of the world must be able to provide a path that allows the youth to attain these freedoms and justices. They must also provide a vision to real freedom and social justice not yet attained by human societies.

The path to real freedom and social/economic justice will need to be lit by humanitarian principles. All people will someday need to question their concepts of freedom:

Does my personal freedom infringe on the freedom of others?

Does my freedom help others to attain the same freedom?

Most important of all:

Does my desire for particular freedoms attune with a larger vision of social/economic equality and prosperity for all?

As stated earlier, freedom of any sort comes with a price. Many of the freedoms that Americans enjoy today—expensive cars and SUV's, overstocked grocery stores, bargain electronic stores, super department stores, lavish homes filled with all the nice gadgets this modern age has unveiled—all come with an underlying social/economic injustice for others somewhere else in the world. When we have more than we need, someone out there is going without. We are all going to have to start asking ourselves about the products we buy and about the things we consume:

Do they come from sustainable, environmentally friendly industry?

Do the businesses that we support have a humanitarian social/economic vision?

Until all individuals begin taking some responsibility for the social/economic condition of the world around them, the potential golden age of prosperity for all of humanity will continue to slip away.

From the beginning of its founding, United Credit could provide a powerful example and guidelines for people to achieve a richer, more meaningful experience of freedom—a freedom that is illuminated by a humanitarian vision of social/economic justice for all. The most powerful example of personal freedom will in fact come from people who have found happiness and success in the act of helping others.

This is the very foundation of United Credit—the core philosophy.

Part 4

United Credit and Social/ Economic Transformation

United Credit and Community Investment

One of the most damaging aspects of modern economic activity is corporate growth. Corporate growth is contrary to community growth. When corporations come into a once successful community economy, they end up siphoning off the economic assets and community wealth in more ways than one. Fast food chains, coffee/donut chains, super department stores, home/hardware supply chains and more are all transforming economic wealth into the hands of a few—those that live outside of and are removed from the communities they are destroying. This type of corporate economic growth robs communities of jobs and small business opportunities—not to mention the vast spectrum of manufacturing jobs lost from the corporate exodus to the third world cheap labor markets. Unregulated corporate growth also robs communities of their creativity and productivity.

The most important aspects of a successful community economy are productivity, pride and shared prosperity. Time after time, I have seen once prosperous, happy business owners, trades people and skilled producers reduced to working for the corporate chains that drove them or their companies out of business. They end up working for 10 or 12 dollars an hour and barely getting by—often suffering from depression and loss. I have been in countless small communities where former business owners now manage the shelves of chain stores! This is not a model of community investment that any social economy can withstand. It borders on the type of economic activities that took place in the feudal societies of the past! It is becoming more and more evident in the world today that the corporate model is a model of human suffering and inherent slavery.

When communities are destroyed economically in these ways, a greater social crisis develops, leading to depression, addiction, health problems, crime, and increased social service/welfare needs, etc. Targeted economic investment into communities is an essential need more than ever, both here in America and in communities around the world. As radical as it may be, boycotting and eventually dismantling corporate chains may be the only way to create meaningful and lasting community economies.

United Credit would focus on community investment by addressing core economic issues.

<u>Community Investment Core Issues:</u>

Homes/shelter
Clean water, healthy/fresh food resources
Accessible health care/clinics
Affordable energy
Disaster preparation
Employment opportunities
Education
Independent public communication and media

The current home mortgage crisis is one of the core issues of social/economic failure and community destruction. The most basic of all human rights—shelter—is being violated in our own country on a scale never before witnessed on the planet. It is extremely important to change the tide of increasing homelessness as soon as possible. The right to not only have a home, but to afford a home is basic and this right should not be perverted into a trading commodity for the wealthy banks and lending institutions—especially those so far removed from the communities they have invaded. United Credit would help homeowners in trouble and create a bank of homes for those in need. The important issue is to instill new ideals about home ownership in communities as soon as possible. We cannot allow the current trend of foreclosures and intimate/personal wealth assets (homes) to be transferred into the hands of a few. If people are willing to work and help others, they should have the right to a home.

Right now, hard working Americans are losing their homes simply because the financial system failed them. Communities are stressed and strained to the limit with rising homelessness. Families are living out of cars and vans. Something is terribly wrong with this picture. We need to put honest, hard working people back into homes, while giving them opportunities to recreate their lives. United Credit would provide opportunities for people to earn the assistance they need by sharing their time, skills, knowledge and abilities with others participating in progressive community projects.

Homes that are sitting vacant, not only should be acquired by humanitarian organizations, they should be retrofitted with more energy efficient heating, hot water and cooling systems. Large homes could be modified into multi-family units. Solar systems could be installed. Ridiculous, oversized lawns could be turned into productive vegetable gardens. There are endless opportunities to create jobs while putting people back into homes.

United Credit could potentially provide the needed humanitarian values, the opportunities, the homes and a new economic rebirth on the community level.

The second major core issue in community investment is clean water and healthy, affordable food. The world is currently heading into major crisis regarding food and water. All communities around the planet are faced with the need to develop ways to solve the coming crisis. By supporting food banks, community gardens, independent farms, and research into better local food options, United Credit could create many opportunities for sustainable economic solutions on the community level. Research has shown that small independent farms are not only more productive and more efficient; they build better, healthier communities while promoting more sustainable long-term farming practices.

The present corporate takeover of America's food supplies is a tragic situation that can have no good outcome. The spread of genetically altered seeds, radiated meats, hormone laced dairy products, and toxic food additives are causing the greatest health epidemic ever to unfold in any society at any time in history. Americans, as well as third world peoples, have become the lab subjects for evil corporations.

A prime example of this type of corporate evil is the mass production and sale of aspartame. Developed as a by-product of chemical warfare during World War II, aspartame is known to be extremely toxic. Corporate lobbyists have repeatedly blocked attempts by educated congressman, scientists, and food safety activists to get aspartame off the market. Yet, in 2011, it is still widely used as a sweetener in diet foods and actually has been shown to be one of the primary causes of obesity! There is evidence that it also destroys the central nervous system and is linked to multiple sclerosis, systemic lupus, methanol toxicity, blindness, seizures, headaches, depression, anxiety, memory loss, birth defects and death.

Education about food safety must play a huge role in community development and there are amazing opportunities yet to be explored in terms of community organic food production—hydroponic gardens, winter greens, greenhouses heated with solar/compost systems. All of these new and exciting opportunities, once established, could be shared throughout the world. Imagine all the new opportunities for work and service that would be created! It sure beats the Peace Corps position that was once offered to me: working as a foreman in a molding factory in the Micronesian Islands—a portable factory that went from island to island stripping trees to make expensive moldings for developed countries, while leaving the island culture decimated of their sacred trees and dependent on monthly surplus food drops! (I turned down that position.)

It is extremely important to support communities in the areas that really need support. This takes some exploration and study into the nature of the community and its strengths and weaknesses. One cannot go into a community and project a vision or ideal that may not fit that community. The Peace Corps has had a long history of doing this around the world and now corporations are doing the same on a greater scale with only their self-interests at heart.

In the areas of food production and management, it is important that every community begin to create food stores and food banks whenever possible. I can envision that an organization, such as United Credit, could ultimately manage a global food bank that could be directly linked to all the world's communities. Communities that have surpluses could donate into the global food bank. Communities that have food deficits could draw from the global food bank. With the current trends of globalization, such a global food bank is the only humanitarian solution to world hunger. In the current global economy, food inequalities and food wasting is rampant. The only real global management being done today is done in commodities/exchange markets for the sake of corporate and/or individual profits. *(The manipulation of rice in the commodities/exchange markets in recent years is a prime example.)* This has to change if there is going to be any long-standing social/community progress. In most cases, what drives societies in the first stages of revolution is hunger!

Access to clean water is already one of the most critical issues facing humanity today. Not only have growing populations put strains on local water resources, corporations have been dumping huge amounts of pollutants that eventually end up in ground water. Water conservation on all levels is also an area that needs concentrated investment—water purification, water saving, etc.

With all of this being said, I envision an organization such as United Credit making huge community investments in healthy food and clean water resources—investments starting at the grass roots local level.

Community investment into assessable health care /local clinics is also critical. How many people are aware that even in Cuba, there are multiple free health clinics in almost every community? Many developed and developing societies around the world see the right to affordable, free healthcare as a basic need. America however, has gone down the barbaric road of capitalistic health care service. Now it is out of control. The number of people in this country with good health care is decreasing, not increasing.

A major focus of United Credit would be to help establish free health care clinics in as many communities as possible. This would be accomplished by combining many aspects of the United Credit charter such as creating opportunities for trades people, doctors, nurses—volunteers from all walks coming together to build, staff and maintain potential clinics. This is not a pipe dream folks! Just 10 hours a week from each person and from a resource of people wanting to help—people earning their own United *credit*. This is going to be the wave of the future. It is not about money anymore. We are coming to an end of an age and the beginning of a new one. Many societies are falling into revolution and change at this moment, while I sit and write this book. Already, people are mobilizing in these torn apart societies to help each other with the basic human need for shelter, food and healthcare. Imagine an organization like United Credit with a vast wealth of human and material resources—coming into needy societies offering opportunities that allow all people to satisfy those basic needs and rights by simply offering their help to others.

Along with the other aspects of community investment mentioned above, United Credit would take the lead in helping to create assessable healthcare and free clinics at the community level.

Affordable energy is a big issue but not unsolvable. The problem is that we are still being spoon fed fossil fuels. That is the fundamental problem that needs to change and would be a major area of focus for United Credit resulting in many new employment opportunities on the community level. Credit for alternative energy systems could be provided. Perhaps credit could even be provided for the local production/development of such systems: credit not in the traditional sense of loans and money, but through United Credit—people and resources, opportunities for employment, exchange of services, etc.

All kinds of alternative energy solutions for small communities could be explored such as solar, solar compost, geothermal, hydrogen and wind.

Despite what we are being led to believe by corporate controlled media, there are many advances and proven successes to all of the above mentioned alternatives in energy generation.

Small projects could potentially grow into bigger projects. A community garden and green house designed with solar compost heating systems could expand to heat area businesses and homes, while providing the organic materials for better and richer garden beds. Programs to help educate people about more efficient ways to use energy—more efficient appliances, vehicles, etc. could be developed, which in turn would create even more economic opportunities on the community level. A whole new economy is in the wings waiting to spring forth from the ashes of this dying one we call money and the *American Dream*. I would be willing to bet my life that once oil and gas dries up and is suddenly not available, the American ingenuity factor would kick in and we would soon have all kinds of alternative energy systems powering our transportation needs!!

The creation of a new and real economy will have to start on the community level and it will come out of the pursuit of sustainable/renewable resources. United Credit would support new and innovative research in all alternative energy fields.

Another area of importance in terms of community investment is the creation of safe havens for potential times of crisis. In this increasingly unstable social/environmental world, it's important that communities have safe places of refuge and shelter. Many employment opportunities could be generated by instituting a program of building refuge shelters equipped with all the supplies needed for temporary survival during times of crisis. These survival centers would have water purification capacities, seed banks, food stocks, emergency communication abilities, medical supplies, etc. It is obvious that humanity has entered uncertain times and United Credit could help communities develop these types of safe emergency shelters.

The creation of and maintenance of emergency shelters could actually serve to bring communities closer together, as well as potentially initiating all kinds of new healthy economic/social activity.

As mentioned earlier, I have been writing for years about the potential planetary crisis developing out of the increased use of fossil fuels. It is bad enough that we are pumping millions of tons of carbon back into the atmosphere; but the real problem created from removing fossil fuels from the earth's crust is rarely discussed in scientific communities. Humanity is destroying the balance of the crustal plates by removing millions of tons of coal, oil and natural gas per day from the continental shelves. The only way nature can attempt to keep the gravitational stability of the crustal plates is to move water and lava around the planet in increasingly more dramatic spurts causing more floods, earthquakes and volcanoes. Thus, future natural disaster preparation is extremely important and United Credit would take the lead in this type of preparation, which as mentioned, could result in sparking all kinds of new economic activity on the community level.

United Credit would support community development in the areas of disaster preparation and survival.

Community investment into education is another core issue. Times are changing and educational opportunities in communities must change to reflect this. First and foremost, once a new humanitarian economic model has begun to be adopted, new educational directions will unfold. Renewed social education of young people could begin as children are encouraged to help others whenever possible. Educational programs and opportunities that foster sustainable living could flourish among children such as practical science labs that produce energy, food, clean water and other products for their families and the community. We have to shift away from the corporate box store mentality. We cannot continue to turn out whole generations of people who are totally removed from the process of creating healthy living! We cannot continue to create whole generations that view their ultimate goal as one of acquiring money and false wealth.

Education on this level is absolutely critical. Humanity is heading for an economic crisis without any backup plan. Millions of children, along with their parents (even in America) are being forced into homelessness and hunger by an out of control capitalist economy. All communities need new educational goals and directions that teach our youth new economic models and alternatives that will foster real economic prosperity. True economic prosperity is all about the basics: food, water, housing, education, healthcare and productive human activity. With new directions in community investment and education, unemployment would quickly become a thing of the past.

Today, in America, education is in trouble. There has been a whole shift into business education in past generations—business education based on economic models of capitalistic growth, profit and accounting methods to count the beans. There has been very little education in the area of moral/

humanitarian economics—virtually no education incorporating a humanitarian vision of the future world economy.

United Credit would make immediate strides to set up new models and exciting opportunities in education on the community level—models that would allow young people to become a real part in the creation and sustaining of new economic opportunities within their community. Educating the youth is the future of humanity.

Independent public media and equal access communication technologies are extremely important issues. Most all news sources are owned and controlled by a handful of wealthy media tycoons that slant their programming and advertising in favor of corporate interests. New opportunities in independent presses, public programming and broadcasting will be fundamental in creating healthier, better informed communities and new economies. Furthermore, communication technologies should not be reserved for just those who can afford them. Part of any new economic model will be the need to address this issue. Free and open access to communication technologies should someday be a basic human right. People should also have the knowledge and freedom to pick and choose these technologies to insure that they are not harming other cultures or the environment during any phase of their development and distribution (such as unlawful or dangerous mining of raw materials, forced labor, environmental destruction, etc.).

United Credit would promote and support independent public media and equal access communication technologies.

In terms of community investment and employment opportunities, United Credit could supply a huge database of services needed with a bank of United credit available to everyone seeking to work or help others and their communities. Within this type of investment by United Credit into any community, there would be a guided vision and plan to create healthy and happy societies—a vision and plan that meets all the basic needs and hopes of those who are part of that community.

Social/Economic Transformation

The implementation of an organization such as United Credit could potentially create the foundation for needed social/economic transformation throughout the world. Most all social economies around the globe are developing without a long term humanitarian vision. They are also developing further and further away from moral and spiritual values regarding human economic activity. Humanity needs organizations/foundations that work to instill a new social/economic vision, as well as new economic values and philosophies. By creating systems of shared wealth, shared resources, shared visions of prosperity, and shared visions of environmental protection, United Credit could become a cornerstone for major social/economic transformation. Currently, there are hundreds of humanitarian/non-profit organizations working around the world. What is needed is an organization that links them all together with a united vision.

It is important that all societies stop and re-examine the real purpose, goals and directions of their economies. They must examine their concepts of economic prosperity. Do their economies favor a few select companies/corporations and leave the majority in debt and struggle? Are their economies meaningful and sustainable without harming the environment or future generations? Economic prosperity needs to be redefined on all levels—locally, nationally and globally. If these issues are not addressed soon, humanity will be forced to address them during times of great social and economic crisis as the capitalistic model continues towards a certain catastrophic death.

Creating economic change and shifts in economic values is not a radical idea, nor would it be a difficult challenge. In reality, society is ripe for such change. People are ready for more purpose and meaning in their lives and people are ready for the type of shared economic prosperity that United Credit proposes. People are desperate to get out from under mountains of debt and worry. People from all the world's societies simply want to have access to basic economic rights, as mentioned throughout this book. But most of all, the collective human soul desires something greater for the future than what our current economic system is creating. United Credit could offer increasing opportunities for people to fulfill their basic needs without creating debt, as well as providing real and meaningful opportunities to help others—a stepping stone to new economic values and beliefs. United Credit could eventually help all economies develop realistic and purposeful visions of economic prosperity for future generations to come.

Without a doubt, there will be great political/corporate resistance to any type of core philosophical change that would discredit and/or dismantle the current models of economic prosperity—models that benefit only a few and that keep the vast majority of people in debt and struggle. Our current political/economic system does not foster humanitarian values, nor does it offer any long-term plan for human prosperity, happiness and ultimate survival on this planet. Change will come in small steps and will evolve from new economic models that start in small communities around the world. In the end, it may be the efforts made by small communities and dedicated non-profit/alternative foundations that guide the world into a new age of real economic prosperity. However, there is a tremendous need for a worldwide organization such as United Credit to mobilize and distribute economic resources through a new value system based on:

- ➢ People helping people
- ➢ People sharing their resources, skills and talents
- ➢ People working towards sustainable economic activity
- ➢ People working towards a real world vision for the future

Humanity is at the most critical crossroad in its history on the planet. Social and economic transformation is going to take place either through peaceful, well-designed change or through upheaval and revolution. We are seeing this happening all over the world. Unfortunately, American politicians—our partisan congress people—are missing the boat. Their inaction, their corporate favoritism and their insensitivities to social problems are actually fostering a potentially violent revolution. America can and should avoid such a revolution. More than any country in the world, America has the resources to create amazing economic change and transformation.

It is not too late to avert such troubled times. There is no need to let our social economy fall into chaos. An organization, such as United Credit, offers real hope and real change right now. It offers a solid solution to the rising unemployment and financial suffering that is increasing in American society.

PROPERTY AND RESOURCE MANAGEMENT

Humans belong to the Earth. The Earth (land, water, forests and minerals) does not belong to humans. This basic philosophy/world view is what has sustained human cultures around the world for thousands and thousands of years. Forests and farmlands have successfully been collectively shared by societies since the earliest days of human history. Only in the past century or two, have the codes of common ownership been challenged; and only in the past decades, has this code been completely disregarded and dissolved in many cases. Corporations have been solidifying their *ownership* of massive tracks of farmland and forest here in America and abroad.

Corporations have also been solidifying their ownership of seeds and native plants (biopiracy) all around the world. How can one individual or corporation file for and be granted a patent on native plants in Indian or South America (or anywhere else in the world)? These plants have been used for medicine or nutrition for thousands of years by Indigenous cultures. What world organization or authority has the right to grant such a patent? Can we allow any *World Trade Organization* to permit such practices which strip societies of their rights to grow, use and market their own native seeds and plants? How ludicrous is the idea that some legalized organization could actually punish and prosecute local farmers or families for doing what their ancestors have done for thousands of years to survive?

The privatization of land, plants, water or any natural resource is a very dangerous path for humanity—a path that has been and will be a dark and dismal end for human societies. There are so many examples that could be mentioned, but the examples of privatization with food and medicine sources are the most dramatic and self-evident. A corporation gaining a patent on corn seeds in a South American community, which uses corn as its basic food source, is a primary example. In recent years, laws and regulations have been written by the World Trade Organization that will ultimately make it a crime for local farmers to grow or market their own native species. Corporations are flooding these societies (through force) with genetically altered seeds and toxic pesticides that GMO seeds are able to withstand. Can you imagine the damage being done to the environment, the water, the wildlife and to humans eating the harvests of these seeds? Can you imagine the economic/ social damage being created in these communities by corporate market control and manipulation?

In all areas of natural resources, privatization has led to corporate greed, environmental and economic destruction. In every example of economic failure in America, private/ corporate ownership can be found as the root cause. Whether it be the agricultural, energy, natural resource, or food industry, the issues of "ownership" and management, in terms of primary resources, needs to be examined and overhauled. New codes of common ownership need to be created. Ancient codes of common ownership need to be revived and enforced. This is one of the most important social/economic rights and one that United Credit would need to confront during its inception as a new economic model.

Once again, this subject flirts with the notion of socialism. While it is true that socialism evolved as a reaction to the problems of private ownership and capitalism, socialist philosophies or movements (and there are many) have never really been founded on or rooted in humanitarian ideals. Socialist philosophies of the modern era deal with the social/ economic issues of production, distribution and exchange of goods, and determine whether these means of economic activity should be privately controlled, state controlled or nationally controlled, etc. Socialism was originally a rejection of rampant capitalism during the industrial revolution and thus has its philosophical roots based in the working class struggle. Socialist philosophies have never fully questioned the concepts of money or the full spectrum of basic economic rights for all people.

Humanity needs to move down a new path guided by real and profound humanitarian codes of economic behavior. Thus we have to move far beyond socialist philosophies into a realm of economic and social activity that is sustainable and fair to all people, all cultures and all nations. We have to move into a realm of economic activity that protects the environment and the natural systems, which give us the opportunity for existence in the first place.

Fair and protective economic practices can and will only evolve out of principles of common use and ownership. Collective management of land and resources will be the root of any humanitarian economic transformation. In conjunction with collective management practices, there will need to be a transformation in our values regarding money and exchange. Currently, the incentive for the destruction of vast land tracks of forests or mineral rich mountains is not for the benefit of humanity but for the benefit of a few wealthy corporations or individuals. If you take money and the concepts of personal wealth out of the equation, societies will ideally be left to collectively manage their local resources for the good of all.

Of course this has not always been the lesson of the past. Growing populations have many times destroyed their forests or their lands through unchecked survival/economic activity. However, humanity is evolving and these are the lessons of living on one planet—one limited ecosystem. These are the social economic lessons that all people in the world today are struggling with. Whether we like it or not, it is going to come down to equal access to clean water, clean air, healthy food, energy resources, shelters, medicine and communication technology. Whether it will be through a designed and conscious change or a turbulent social upheaval, material equality and environmental protection will have to be some of the central core philosophies of any new economic models.

Not-for-profit management of property and resources is going to be a critical and needed shift in areas of human economic activity. Community co-operatives will be very important in any attempt to create new economic activity. In areas of food storage and distribution, housing, energy, education and healthcare, co-ownership, co-operation and community sharing are the basic building blocks of sustainable economic values. On the larger scale, world co-operatives could help create fair and equitable distribution of food and resources from country to country. Unlike the World Bank and The World Trade Organization, a *world co-operative* would not have policies of putting countries in debt or forcing them to accept corporate privatization of their lands or resources. A world co-operative would be set up to help countries by balancing and sharing available food, resources, sustainable technologies and knowledge.

A World without Money?

How did the current economic age of money begin? Where did humanity go wrong? Perhaps we are just evolving out of a primitive material consciousness. Perhaps we are devolving back to a primitive state of selfishness and greed. Whatever the case may be, the behavior of human beings in the past few thousand years is not a reflection of the natural world we live in. Nowhere in nature do we see animals hoarding resources to the degree that we humans do thereby destroying their communities or environments.

The examples of negative human behavior that abound on the planet today clearly push the edge of greed and selfishness to the level of pure evil—all driven by the quest for money. If you take money out of the equation, then much of the evil cannot exist. For example: the drug dealer who is destroying thousands of lives or the pimp who is prostituting dozens of woman would have no reason to behave or act out these dramas if it were not for the quest of money. Take money out of the equation and much of the greed and evil we see in the world today would dry up and vanish. The arms industry would crash, the pharmaceutical companies would transform, corrupt politicians would disappear and the destruction of our planet would end. If there is no spiritual, moral or ethical record of economic commerce, then crime, greed and inhumanity will mushroom continuously.

Whether we are ready for it or not, we are going to eventually be living in a world without money. The world economy is crashing. The economic system that humanity is operating from has absolutely no moral or spiritual foundation. What are our visions for the future? What would a world without money look like—and if it looks like a possible reality, how do we get there from here? It is time to stop in our tracks right now and ask these questions. The collective human soul is advancing beyond the concepts of money—a process that is in motion and cannot be turned back.

A world without money will be a world of shared resources, shared educational/creative opportunities and shared vision for economic prosperity for humans on this planet. Humanity is quickly moving towards full-scale globalization on every level. There are only two possible outcomes of globalization: The first one, the outcome we seem to be heading towards, is a militarized state with a select wealthy handful of people who control the world's food supplies, energy resources, communication technology, etc. That is the natural progression of our current economic system and the widespread faith in an inherently valueless currency.

The second possible outcome of globalization is something in the order of a new economic value system base on humanitarian principles that is promoted and enforced by an International Economic Congress. Such an International Economic Congress would need to be supported by all nations and all peoples—protecting the social/economic rights of all people, as well as promoting sustainable, environmental friendly policies, and insuring the equitable distribution of the planet's natural wealth and resources. The longer it takes humanity to get a handle on the escalating process of globalization, the harder it's going to be to create the second, most desirable outcome of economic peace and prosperity for all nations.

As mentioned above, a world without money is a world with much less crime—a world with much less corruption. If humanity shifts to a new economic model and value system —one that is based on our actions of giving and sharing—the monetary system as we know it, along with all its faces of greed and selfishness, will begin to fade into the past. When you have an economy driven with money—money that is linked to nothing real, nothing moral or spiritual—you have an economy that is subject to every conceivable evil and injustice that humans could possibly drum up. This is what we have seen all throughout the history of our money-driven societies and this is what we are certainly seeing today.

The process of the social economy is not meant to be about the amassing of wealth by a few. It is meant to be about taking care of its entire people—the whole of society. The concepts of equality that are written in the American Constitution need to be developed further in the areas of economic equality.

A world without money will be a different world for sure but it will be a better world. What do all people really want during their passage through these short lifetimes? What they really want is peace, prosperity, enough food, a warm home, family, friends, love, adventure and the quest for knowledge. Greed and the misguided quest for money get in the way of all that. Societies are capable of providing all of the things people really want and need through co-operation and shared resources. We have seen this in times of catastrophe and tragedy in various communities around this country and the world. Humans have proven their capability to rise above the concepts and bounds of the current monetary economy when it comes to helping people in desperate need.

The money driven economy of America at this moment in time has become a complete charade of madness. According to recent statistics, twenty million foreclosed American homes are sitting empty while hundreds of thousands of hardworking American families are forced into homelessness. I do not care what anyone tries to say to justify such a scenario. It is a crime committed against the very ideals of this country—against all the people who have worked hard and died for this country in the past. Countless money-madness crimes are being committed in this country and around this world against innocent people, young and old—jobs taken away from historically hard working communities in America and sent to places in the world where exploitation, child slavery and environmental destruction run rampant—young women abducted and forced into the sexual slave trade industry and wars instigated by corporations and corrupt political leaders for profit and the amassing of personal wealth. This is nothing new though. The history of money in the past few thousand years is full of the same mad crimes. I feel that humanity is now reaching the breaking point.

The value system of money today is an absolute false reality with no intrinsic human value. This money is created out of thin air and released out into an economic system that has no sound moral/ethical foundation. This is the most important reason why our economic values need to shift. By relating economic values—our mediums of exchange—to real and meaningful human action (work, service, humanitarianism), all human economy becomes an absolute positive social reform.

One might argue that there is no difference if an individual is paid one hundred dollars for ten hours of work or one hundred credit units with an organization like United Credit. Well, here is the difference: The one hundred dollars might allow a person to pay a bill or get something that they need, but that one hundred dollars is quickly sucked up into an economy that is basically transferring all the social, material and resource wealth into the hands of a few. Those one hundred dollars came and went without leaving behind one ounce of dignity or pride with that individual.

However, the individual that receives one hundred credit units from the United Credit foundation has the potential to not only have their material needs met, they know the history of those credit units—credit units which were earned while being part of a purposeful social economy that is dedicated to fairness and equality—something to be proud of! More importantly, when those credit units are redeemed, their intrinsic value can only be used to create more economic equity in society. Their **real** value is contrary to the **false** value of money.

A world without money would be a different world. Instead of the youth of this developed world coming out of educational facilities into financial debt, stress, worry and/ or unemploy-ment, they should be coming out of educational facilities already actively participating in the world economy in satisfying and meaningful ways. The youth of the world today are coming into an economy that expects them to have an apartment, a cell phone, credit cards, motor vehicle, insurance and all the other alluring materials things that are common to our developed societies. All this being said, how many of these youth have ever been given opportunities to fulfill their material needs through some sort of meaningful social service or community involvement? Not many I expect.

For example, societies like the United Kingdom are faced with a horrendous social problem along these lines—20% unemployment among the youth with no direction or opportunity to create any kind of meaningful economic activity at all. This is a prime example of a failing society in desperate need of an organization such as United Credit. The United States is not far behind. Unemployment is on the rise and there are no real investments into sustainable job creation by either the private or government sectors of society.

In a world without money, there would be no unemployment. Opportunities to help others are abundant and all around us. The current capitalistic economic model does not support these abundant opportunities. While there are many non-profit and humanitarian organizations operating within our society, how many people are able to escape the cycles of debt and worry about money to be free to give of their time to these organizations? Once people fall on hard times, there are almost no options to begin immediate work with an organization that could insure that their needs would be fulfilled. The more the unemployed fall into despair and hopelessness, the more likely our society, as a whole, will begin to crumble.

A world without money will be a world of changing consciousness—changing economics and economies. People will eventually come to understand that our work and service in society is not really about how much we can take from society or how much we can amass for ourselves. Our work and service in society is about helping to insure that all people have the same opportunities and material comforts that we desire. Our current corporate and political leaders are so far removed from the ordinary realities of everyday Americans that they have lost their compassion and humanitarianism, yet they expect continued unquestioned support. This is all changing.

All around the world, societies are rising up and demanding economic fairness, material equality and accountability. As mentioned earlier, humanity is evolving whether we like it or not. The pull towards new economic models is very strong and growing stronger by the month. The world needs economic visionaries—people who can see what a world without money might look like. United Credit offers a visionary bridge towards a more just and equalized world economy.

Economy verses Environment

The world economy of today is literally at war with our environment—our planet's ecosystem. For every inch of economic or technological advancement gained, a mile of the earth's atmosphere, mineral resources, forests and natural species is lost. There is absolutely no global vision indicating where all of this is going to lead humanity. The real change that all humans and all cultures are facing is change in our economic activity. The current economic practices are heading for a doomsday end. Oil will run out, forests will be wiped out, our soil will be desolate, ocean life will perish and our atmosphere will no longer be able to sustain life.

Any new economic activity initiated by communities, states or nations must be accompanied by policies of environmental sustainability. Any economic Bill of Rights must incorporate articles of environmental protection. Environmental protection is not just protecting land, water, forests, etc. Environmental protection must be extended to protect the circumstances and conditions where all humans live and work; non-toxic work places, non-toxic construction materials, better air filtration and ventilation, etc. Protecting the environment is not just an ecological issue; it is a very important social issue as well. Protecting the environment also means protecting communities and societies.

A prime example of economic/social failure on an unprecedented scale is the mining in the African Congo. Corporate economic greed has led to the wide spread selling of arms and political/rebel conflict. It has led to the raping of women and children, slavery and torture—all for the quest of diamonds, and more recently, the precious metals used in cell phone technology. Humanity is in serious spiritual and moral trouble. The failing societies around the world are just a reflection of our failed social/economic philosophies.

If we are going to change our economic/social behavior, it has got to start with such issues as the one mentioned above. If I am going to use a cell phone laced with precious metals from the Congo, then I want to know that those environments, communities and peoples of the Congo are benefiting with sustainable economic/social activity as well as sustainable environmental practices. I am talking about radical changes in how we create economic activity but it is these radical changes that will save humanity and the future of human life on this planet.

We are in the end times in many ways. I see these end times as the end of an age of greed and economic disharmony. But I also see these times as the beginning of a new age of potential economic prosperity for all. Globalization has only two ends as mentioned previously. Either we create social/economic equity and sustainability, or we end up in chaos, war and economic/environmental destruction.

On the community level, practical and realistic economic change could be implemented by an organization such as United Credit; economic change that takes into account the local natural environment and the local working and living environments of individuals. Economic activity can no longer be pitted against these environments. Economies must work in harmony with all environmental and social concerns.

Americans are being led down the road of complete corporate domination, destruction and pollution of their local/national environments and food sources. American corporations are spreading this behavior to as many countries as they can in an attempt to control land, water and food for the sake of huge profits and gain.

However, there are many communities around the world that are already making substantial social/economic changes in order to protect their local environments, water supplies, crop diversity and seeds. Many countries are now taking steps to outlaw the destructive practices of American corporations that are trying to proliferate genetically modified seeds, chemical fertilizers and toxic pesticides across the planet.

There is no doubt that humanity is at a serious crossroad in terms of economy verses environment. Any and all new economic models, philosophies, codes, constitutions, etc. will have to first and foremost take into consideration environmental and sustainability issues of local communities, as well as the future of the entire global community. The prognosis at the moment is not good considering the amount of control that wealthy corporations are exercising within the current global banks, world trade institutions and military/political forces. What is it going to take to make radical changes in the political/economic philosophies and policies of these corporations?

Part 5

United Credit: The Foundation

The Mission Statements:

To create and sustain a new economic/philosophic model based on the actual deeds and meaningful human actions of sharing and working towards a common humanitarian vision of peace and prosperity for all.

To eventually remove paper (valueless) money from community-based economies and replace it with a form of economic compensation that is rich with human purpose, social/economic equality and humanitarian advancement.

Does this sound pretty idealistic? Not really. When you come right down to it and strip away money and the perceived concepts of money, humans still have the same needs, wants and desires. People still need food and shelter. People still desire learning. They still desire happiness and fulfillment. All the resources are around us. All the knowledge, talent and skill are around us. It is all within us. We are the creators of this reality. This reality is not creating us.

It is all a matter of conception—what we are taught and how we are conditioned. The truth is that all human beings are heart-centered humanitarians at their core. One or two generations of re-education and reconditioning within new humanitarian economic models will most definitely produce a better world. Once again, it is possible to create a *free* society that prints no money, exchanges no money or amasses no money. It is possible to create a society that manages the collective resources in a fair and equitable way allowing each person the same freedoms enjoyed by all others.

UNITED CREDIT: THE VISION

It would be realistic to envision small communities around this country and the world developing new economic models like the one proposed through United Credit. I can easily envision a foundation such as United Credit transforming a small, struggling community into a thriving new economy. Imagine a small town in the Midwest—a town that has lost all its jobs to cheap foreign sweatshops, 50% unemployment, failing city and social services, rampant depression and hopelessness. Unemployed people sitting home thinking that they have no hope to change their realities could be given amazing opportunities—opportunities which could result in improving the lives of others in their community. In exchange for their service, United Credit would begin to pro-vide for them in ways they had never thought were possible.

From there I envision people working to make the community a better and healthier place to live with United Credit providing many or all of the opportunities mentioned throughout this book—free health care, education, new economic projects that result in healthy, sustainable communities. Eventually, all of this could become possible without even one dollar ever changing hands between community members and United Credit.

I envision people and communities working together sharing their resources, their skills and their knowledge—people and communities that really reach out to all people across the spectrum to make sure that everyone is getting equal opportunities to have their most basic needs fulfilled. There are organizations all across this country and around this world that are making what progress they can towards such goals; but I envision United Credit working to link all of these organizations together.

I envision the youth of this country and young people around the world excited and inspired by such an organization as United Credit, since the opportunities to transform social economies would be endless—all facilitated by acts of human kindness, sharing, compassion and humanitarian vision. I envision opportunities to transform the social economies through research, science, alternative energy projects and organic farming. I envision new educational opportunities for our youth—live communication links with other communities around the world sharing knowledge and skills.

I don't think that many people realize the powerful transformation in social media going on in the world today. This is the very foundation that is going to help facilitate economic change on a global scale. The youth around the world are driving this communication technology. In many cases, the incoming youth are revolutionizing communication technology. Because of this, great shifts in world economics are inevitable.

Humanity is deeply entrenched in this capitalistic economic system. It is not going to be an easy shift into any new economic model but we have to start somewhere. We have to begin creating bridges to new social economies. There is going to be turmoil and there is going to be chaos and violence; however, I envision social justice as the prevailing force or movement in the end.

UNITED CREDIT: SETTING UP THE FOUNDATION

Beyond creating a non-profit organization, United Credit would be founded on a new economic philosophy as outlined in this book. Furthermore, adopting an economic *Bill of Rights* would serve to guide and shape the foundation as it expanded from small communities to states and nations. Adopting economic goals and guidelines for the developers and administrators of United Credit would be equally as important. For example: compensation for service that excludes money transactions for United Credit administrators.

In the early stages of United Credit, discussing new ideas, sharing United Credit philosophy and expanding information would help to create a growing reserve of food, housing, other material resources and an expanding donor base. As mentioned before, any economic shift would require starting from a money-based world economy. However, any and all money coming into the foundation would be used only to create a solid reserve of material, educational and healthcare resources with the infrastructure to manage and distribute them. Money would also be used to help create new infrastructure and job opportunities for communities to move towards sustainable economic activity on all levels.

Money would never be paid out in exchange for service. This is a very important point, as developed throughout this book. Compensation for work and service can be given in more meaningful, long-term humanitarian ways: debt dissolution, healthier food, housing and individual/community development projects. United Credit would reach out to all those in need on so many levels—not by just handing out assistance but by creating opportunities for people to transform their lives and their communities—thus transforming their economies.

The bottom line is this: United Credit would challenge the concepts of personal gain and profit on all levels—especially in areas of housing, food, energy, education and healthcare. These areas of human economic activity should be considered basic rights for all and the resources available within such economic activity should be available on an equal basis to all people.

Important primary goals of United Credit:

Secure funds to develop and distribute information, books and other materials that promote the United Credit foundation

Solicit members: people who support United Credit philosophy as well as people and organizations already working to transform human economy

Create a Charter/Articles of Incorporation or rules and regulations of United Credit operations—including an Economic Bill of Rights for all people

Create a legal non-profit organization according to all current Federal, State and local regulations

Create a humanitarian-centered management plan as well as a plan for compensation for all United Credit members—one that does not disperse money

Solicit donors; create food banks, housing banks, health care banks, etc.

Solicit businesses, organizations and institutions that need help /human services, while creating data banks of these needs

Offer all people equal opportunities to be a part of the United Credit foundation: provide United Credit *service/compensation* cards

Develop model communities with the focus on new economic activities that move away from money/debt economies; develop ***debt-relief*** strategies

Begin to focus quickly on sustainable economic/environmental activity

Solicit corporations; create a system to rate corporations in terms of their social, environmental and economic responsibility

Work towards an International economic equality—promote the creation of an International Economic Congress founded on a proven/tested Economic Bill of Rights

To become a part of United Credit, in any capacity, please visit:

unitedcrediteconomy.org

Or contact Red Bear Press at:

192 Main Street, Suite 8
Ellsworth, Maine 04605

A Personal Note from the Author

It has been no easy challenge to take on a writing project such as this one, nor will it be easy to embark on the challenge of creating a foundation such as United Credit.

I have been a seeker and a creator of many things; art, music, sculptures, homes, books, gardens and much more. However, I have never been attached to this material world. I realized early on that we are stewards passing through and that we are meant to leave the world a better place—even if only our backyard. I can remember the first home I bought; the home where my two sons were raised. The land had beautiful forests, but the ground was trashed with rubbish, tires, glass and everything else you could imagine. I had a vision that that land would someday be clean and that my children could walk barefoot on a renewed forest floor. Week after week, year after year, I cleaned up the land and planted gardens where I could. We had pumpkin fields and grew organic food. I renewed the old house and built an art studio addition. I designed it so people coming to visit had to walk through the art studio to enter the house. I built tree houses, a basketball court, a wood shop—all places for my children and neighborhood children to play and explore their creative potential. Mostly, this has been the tone of my life—cleaning up environments, planting gardens and creating beauty in sometimes unforgiving conditions.

We are living in an unforgiving economic calamity. Now is the time to create new ideas and examples of real economic prosperity—prosperity that is equally shared among communities, states and nations. The creation of a United Credit economy will consume much of the time I have left in this life passage.